THE WHITETAIL HUNTER'S ALMANAC
7th Edition

by

Dr. Ken Nordberg

Cover by Buzz Buczynski
Photographs & Illustrations by
Jene Kathryn Armstrong & Dr. Ken Nordberg
Edited by Jennifer J. O'Donnell

Published by
SHINGLE CREEK OUTDOOR PUBLICATIONS
MINNEAPOLIS

Copyright © 1994 by Shingle Creek Outdoor Productions
All rights reserved
LIBRARY OF CONGRESS CATALOG CARD NUMBER:
ISSN 1046-3097
Manufactured in the United States of America

Dedication

To my sister,

Carole

CONTENTS

Introduction	1
Chapter 1: Johnny-on-the-Spot Buck Hunting	5
Definition	5
Development	5
Key on Vulnerable Deer	14
Scout Daily	15
Quickly Hunt Vulnerable Deer	16
Effectiveness	16
Step 1: Pre-Season Scouting	19
Locating 2–3 Suitable Quarries	23
Locating Mid-Hunt Scouting Areas and Approaches — Range Element Scouting	29
Identifying Buck Range Elements	34
Likeliest Current Locations and Next Destinations of Adult Bucks	36
Locating and Identifying Range Elements of Adult Bucks	42
Adult Buck Bedding Areas	43
Dominant Buck Bedding Areas	48
Lesser Adult Buck Bedding Areas	49
Lesser Adult Buck Bedding Areas During Rut Phases II and III	49
Adult Buck Feeding Areas	50
Principle Feeding Areas of Adult Bucks	56
Principle Feeding Area No. 1	56
Principle Feeding Area No. 2	57
Principle Feeding Area No. 3	58
Principle Feeding Area No. 4	61
Principle Feeding Area No. 5	61
Post-Storm Feeding Areas	62
Adult Buck Watering Spots	63
Trails Frequented by Adult Bucks	63
Buck Scrape Trails	66
Adult Doe Range Elements	68
Adult DoeBedding Areas	68
Adult Doe Feeding Areas	69
Adult Doe Watering Spots	71
Minimizing Changes in Buck Range Utilization Attributable to Hunting	71

Locating Approaches to Mid–Hunt Scouting Areas	72
Locating Probable Stand Sites and Approaches	73
Selecting a Stand Site for Opening Morning	80
Step 2: The Opening Half-Day Hunt	83
Last–Minute Mini-Scouting	83
Adjusting to Opening Morning Weather	85
Using a Stool for Whitetail Hunting	85
How to Make a Portable Stool Suitable for Whitetail Hunting	87
The Perilous Journey to Your Stand Site	94
Success vs Non-Success	97
Step 3: Daily Scouting	99
When to Scout	100
Where to Scout	102
How to Scout	104
Be Prepared to Shoot	105
Caught by Surprise	106
Step 4: A Succession of Half-Day Hunts	107
Chapter 2: On the Trail of a Wounded Buck	111
Chapter 3: Cover-All-Bases Buck Hunting	121
Chapter 4: Antler Mountain Showdown	123
Chapter 5: Attacked by a White-tailed Buck	139
Chapter 6: Lyme Disease	143
Epilogue: Cry of the Fawn	146

Acknowledgements

A "special" thanks to:

Buzz Buczynski, friend and artist extraordinaire who again captured the spirit of this book on the cover and conjured up a special brand of darkroom wizardry to make difficult but vital photography publishable.

Jene Kathryn Armstrong, more-than-"special" partner, research and publishing assistant, skilled wildlife photographer and tamer of wild creatures. Most of the photographs in this book are hers, including her wonderful closeups of wolves.

John Nordberg (Nordberg Consulting, 8700 Shiloh Court, Eden Prarie, MN 55437) for producing computer-perfect maps for this book.

Many wolves and wild deer of North America, including kingly bucks, that came to regard Jene and myself as harmless creatures —some of which lost their lives to other hunters as a result—thus greatly reducing the time necessary to develop and establish the effectiveness of hunting methods presented in this book.

x

Author's Introduction

"Wouldn't it be great," I thought, "if I could somehow combine the best of what wolves (the most proficient deer hunters in the world) do to take whitetails with portable stump hunting (a hunting method that makes it extremely difficult for whitetails to identify and avoid human hunters and considerably reduces the likelihood of range abandonment by adult bucks and other deer). What a hunting method that would be."

Well I did it. I not only developed a one-on-one approach, "Johnny-on-the-spot buck hunting," but a small-group approach, "cover-all-bases buck hunting."

These two new hunting methods will not enable you to take an adult buck, the most wary of today's more elusive whitetails, in every attempt. Even wolves can't do that. But they will put you within one-hundred yards of one or more adult bucks during nearly every half-day of hunting. Using traditional hunting methods, the average hunter's odds for taking one adult buck per hunting season are only about 1-in-30. Using either or both of these new hunting methods, the odds are nearly 1-in-1.

These hunting methods evolved in consequence of a startling discovery made five years ago: almost everything the average hunter does to prepare to hunt whitetails these days, including pre-season scouting, selecting and preparing stand sites and formulating hunting plans based on pre-season scouting, is only effective for one-half to two days of hunting. Once today's adult whitetails realize they are being hunted by humans, typically occurring within one to four whitetail feeding cycles, they abruptly become super-alert, super-cautious and super-stealthy. They begin using cover and terrain that makes them much more difficult to discover or approach without warning. They begin avoiding trails and sites frequented by hunters (identified via sight, sound or scent, including trail scent) and, if necessary, they temporarily abandon their home ranges, or portions of them, and/or avoid moving during daylight hours (become nocturnal). This is why hunting success drops off dramatically after the first one or two days of a hunting season; why more than 90% of whitetails taken by average hunters are inept fawns and yearlings.

This book will teach you to how to hunt super-alert, super-cautious, super-stealthy, adult bucks that know they are being hunted. It will teach you how to outfox the biggest and most wary bucks in your hunting area, day-one, day-two, day-fifteen or day-thirty. It will teach you all this via accounts of long-term, scientifically-based studies of whitetails and wolves and actual hunts, using maps and photos to illustrate tactics used by actual adult bucks to avoid actual hunters and how my hunting partners and I successfully countered these tactics using the hunting methods presented in the book.

This book will also introduce you to a vastly different approach to whitetail hunting. You will learn how to very quickly adapt your hunting to whatever your quarry is doing right now, today, rather than to what it was doing days, weeks or months earlier or what you believe or merely hope it will be doing days, weeks or months in the future. Using this approach, you will eliminate guess-work. You will learn how to know exactly where to hunt, half-day after half-day.

Once you have tried "Johnny-on-the-Spot Buck Hunting," a one-on-one hunting method, and "Cover-All-Bases Buck Hunting," a small-group hunting method, I am certain they will become your favorite hunting methods. They were originally developed to counter much-studied avoidance tactics of super-elusive, wolf-country bucks, but as you will happily discover, they are even more effective for hunting other, less-elusive classes of whitetails, namely adult does, yearlings (including bucks) and fawns. Like "The Gentle Nudge," the very effective, two or three-man hunting method introduced in *Whitetail Hunter's Almanac, 6th Edition*, both of these new hunting methods are variations of "Portable Stump Hunting," the ground-level stand hunting method introduced in *Whitetail Hunter's Almanac, 5th Edition*.

Most of what you will learn evolved from recent studies of adult bucks and wolves near the Canadian Border of Minnesota. The wolves deserve most of the credit. Because they quickly became tame in my presence, I often enjoyed the good fortune of observing them in the act of hunting whitetails. Equally important, I often enjoyed the good fortune of observing whitetails responding to various behavior patterns of wolves. Such observations not only provided great insight into the tactics often used by whitetails to avoid human hunters, but they taught me to recognize the signs characteristic of wolf-deer encounters, enabling me to more quickly amass the information necessary to develop these hunting methods.

Being over-abundant, the wolves of this region are obliged to hunt whitetails year-around, night and day. This has made the surviving deer, especially the adult bucks, the most wary whitetails I have ever studied and hunted. Though a frustration at first, such wariness proved to be a windfall. Ordinarily, to determine whether one hunting method has superiority over another, it is necessary to keep track of numbers, classes and responses of deer spotted over a considerable number of years. It took ten hunting seasons, for example, to become certain of the superiority of "mobile stand hunting," introduced in *Whitetail Hunter's Almanac, 3rd Edition.* In my wolf-country study area the relative effectiveness of a new hunting method becomes obvious in a matter of days. Here, if one or more adult bucks are encountered at short range within a day or two, the method obviously works, or is worthy of further study, and if none are encountered within that time, it doesn't work. "All or nothing" responses of our adult bucks made it possible to repeatedly test a great number different approaches to promising hunting methods and establish with certainty the superiority of the two hunting methods presented in this book within only five hunting seasons.

If you have read any of my other books (*Whitetail Hunter's Almanacs*), you have become accustomed to thinking and hunting in ways that are quite different—startling departures from tradition. You doubtless have also become accustomed to much improved hunting success, the best yet to come.

If you are a first-time reader, as others before you have discovered, startling departures from tradition are soon subjected to negative peer pressure and resistance to change. To effectively combat it, you need to be made aware of it.

Keep in mind, twenty-million American deer hunters can not only be wrong, but they are often wrong, simply because hardly any of them spend any significant time in our wilds studying whitetails (including writers, speakers and those who sell hunting products). Just because other hunters believe otherwise, do not be dissuaded from using any of the information and methods presented in this book. In time, those who kid you for thinking and doing things differently will be begging you for advice.

Also keep in mind, resistance to change is human nature. It's true of you and it's true of me, and we deer hunters dearly love our old traditions. The trouble is, our old traditional hunting methods have never been particularly effective for taking adult bucks, and they are rapidly becoming even less effective. I resisted and doubted my own research findings every step of the way, but I eventually gave in to change because I wanted to be a regularly successful buck hunter. As you read this book, you will also resist and doubt and you will dream up ways of using information and/or instructions provided in an attempt to improve your own current favorite hunting method, not materially changing the way you hunt deer. If you do this, however, or if you change things or adopt mere half-measures, your hunting success is unlikely to improve. I know because during the years-long process of developing these new hunting methods, I tried every imaginable variation, and via considerable trial and error, I made every conceivable mistake, sometimes by design. What I finally ended up with was judged statistically superior not by me or any other human, but by a considerable number of wolf country adult bucks. Having studied whitetails over much of North America, I know there are no tougher judges anywhere.

Thus, don't worry about what other, less-informed hunters might say and don't waste your valuable hunting time making the same mistakes I made. Do it all, exactly as explained, right from the outset.

A camo headnet, a silent, portable stool, a seated position, natural, unaltered screening cover, a ground level stand site used no more than one-half day and very fresh tracks and/or droppings of a selected quarry 10–50 yards upwind—the elements that make the Johnny-on-the-spot approach extraordinarily effective for hunting the most elusive of whitetails, adult bucks.

Chapter 1

Johnny-on-the-Spot Buck Hunting

Definition

Johnny-on-the-spot buck hunting is a hunting method that enables the hunter to be within 100 yards of one or more adult bucks during almost every half-day of hunting. It consists of four steps: 1) pre-season scouting, 2) the opening morning hunt, 3) daily scouting and, until successful, 4) a succession of half-day hunts. Though applicable to group hunting and hunting all classes of whitetails, this hunting method was originally developed with one goal in mind: to provide a more productive means of hunting super-elusive adult bucks one-on-one (one hunter vs one preselected adult buck). Though basically a stand hunting method, it is very different from conventional stand hunting. The hunter uses two new ground-level stand sites per day, each 10–50 yards from a trail or site used by an intended quarry during the previous 6–24 hours. To find such sites, the hunter scouts daily while hunting.

Development

Now when I think about it, the seed that led me to develop this hunting method was planted the first season I hunted whitetails, nearly fifty years ago. It happened the day my Uncle Jack shot a deer, after which my Uncle Veikko commented, "He was in the right place at the right time."

"How can *I* find the right place at the right time?" I asked Veikko. He laughed and answered, "No one knows how to find it, but when you're there, you sure know it."

After asking many experienced hunters this same question, I finally decided the only way to find an acceptable answer was figure it out myself.

Thus, while tending a five-mile-long weasel trapline at the rambunctious age of ten, I began following deer tracks in snow, believing they would provide the answer. Though unwittingly on the right path, following deer tracks back then did not likely improve my hunting success (considered "lucky," maybe it did), but, to me, it was fascinating and fun.

Twenty-five years later (the summer of 1970) I still did not have the answer, nor did anyone else I knew. Now I really needed it. My oldest son and daughter would soon begin their first season of whitetail hunting. I wanted them to be thoroughly smitten, to anxiously look forward to the next hunting season and every hunting season thereafter. I wanted to ignite the spark that would enrich their lives as much as it had enriched mine. I wanted to establish a family tradition that would thenceforth bring us together in deer camp each fall for the rest of our lives. I was therefore determined they would be successful during their first hunts. I knew it would be difficult. Deer numbers were at a record low and only antlered bucks could be taken. I scouted as I had never scouted before, and discovered more of what I didn't understand than I had ever discovered before. Over and over again I found myself thinking, "If I knew why deer made these signs, I'd have something predictable to exploit." But scouting alone failed to yield anything concrete. If anything, it only added to my confusion. "If I could actually watch whitetails making these signs, compiling enough observations of deer responding to various stimuli under similar circumstances, thus making my findings scientifically "correct," or "truthful," I began thinking, "I'd surely learn what I need to know. If I used a great number of tree stands (tree stands were practically unknown back then) to watch deer during the off-season, I think it could be done." I began with a fervor that even surprised me. Having college degrees in related subjects such Animal Psychology and Zoology, and having many years of experience in physiological research, it seemed as if this was what I was meant to do. In time I became convinced. Thus was born the spare-time hobby that blossomed into my full-time work.

Three years later (1973), I thought I had it all figured out. My hunting partners (including three children) and I were enjoying great buck hunting success despite low deer numbers, oblivious of the fact that our unusual success was primarily attributable to the whitetail's temporary inability to identify hunters in elevated stands (as low as six feet above the ground). Then buck lures entered the picture, those containing doe-in-estrus pheromone the best of them. The right place at the right time became almost anywhere and anytime a bottle of one of these odoriferous potions was opened. All you had to do was make certain you were less than 200 yards upwind of a buck. Within a surprisingly short period of time, however, whitetails, especially adult bucks, learned to recognize and avoid hunters using elevated stands and buck lures, and suddenly I found myself back where I began forty-four years earlier. Well, almost.

My first twenty years of scientifically-based studies provided the important basics: habits and behavior, effects of weather, hunting and changing seasons, phases of the rut, meanings of more than two-hundred deer signs and such. These, in turn, made whitetail classes (5) predictable. Being able to predict where whitetails are located at any one time, and what they are doing, is an enormous asset to hunting, at least theoretically. That was the frustrating part of it. No matter how I tried to apply this hard-won knowledge to traditional hunting methods, it did not appreciably improve hunting success. Such knowledge could not overcome human handicaps—inadequate stealth, relatively poor eyesight and hearing, and for all practical purposes, no sense of smell. It did not appreciably lessen the ability of whitetails to identify and avoid human hunters. I then realized I needed to develop new and better ways to hunt whitetails, means of hunting that would enable human hunters to more regularly exploit whitetail predictability, counter their increasingly effective avoidance tactics and eliminate or reduce the negative effects of incurable human shortcomings.

Five years ago, with the aid of my family of avid deer hunters, I began a massive comparative study of hunting methods, recording numbers, classes and actions of deer seen within effective shooting range. I fully expected many long years would pass before this undertaking would yield significant results. Much to my surprise a special hunting method I had been dickering with for some twenty years, a method that combined the best of still-hunting and the best of stand hunting, eliminating the worst of each, immediately yielded nearly three-times more sightings of unsuspecting deer within 50 yards than all other hunting methods.

The next logical step was to determine why this particular hunting method was so superior. The answers, I felt, would not only provide direction for making improvements, but provide insight into determining whether or not this new hunting method was merely providing us with a means of taking advantage of another temporary whitetail vulnerability. Would whitetails learn to counter it or would it stand the test of time?

In the misty background loomed that old question, "Where is the right place at the right time." Somehow, this new hunting method was putting us in the right place at right time three-times more frequently than other hunting methods. There had to be one or more reasons. If I could discover those reasons, I figured I'd at last have the key to this lifelong enigma.

The answers began to come into focus the day our resident timber wolves (gray wolves) decided I was harmless. From that day forth, I saw them frequently, sometimes daily, occasionally even finding myself in the middle of their hunts. Awed, I soon came to the conclusion gray wolves are the most proficient whitetail hunters in the world.

These wolves hunt whitetails, spring, summer fall and winter. Wherever and whenever I wander within my four-square-mile study area, I find tracks characteristic of their hunting, parts of deer bones from recent kills and fresh wolf droppings loaded with deer hair and sometimes teeth and portions of hoofs of whitetails.

At first I considered these wolves a terrible scourge, the reason the adult bucks in the area were especially wise to ambushes (human stand hunting). Here, dominant bucks were virtually impossible to observe (study) or hunt from tree stands. Then one day, while hunting (using a portable stool at ground level), the resident wolfpack made its first short-range appearance. Though I didn't realize it until it was all over, I happened to be sitting exactly where five of the six-member pack planned to ambush a deer driven to them by the alpha female (the mother of the grown pups). Since then, I have been a gaping spectator of similar hunts on quite a few occasions. The following is typical of such a hunt.

The adult doe, ravenously nipping off tips of red osier branches, suddenly swung her head to her left and froze, eyes, ears and nose trained on the line of dense balsams bordering the beaver pond 200 yards west. After about 30 seconds of intense study, the doe flicked her tail from side-to-side, indicating she had decided "all is secure," and then moved ten yards to another clump of osiers, resuming her ravenous feeding. As if tethered to her tail by a foot-long length of invisible rope, a 305-pound, 10-point dominant buck moved with her, head low, muzzle up, its mouth open and often moving as if drinking the pheromone laden air emitted by the doe (carried to the air via urine), now obviously in estrus. Maintaining an interval of roughly 20 yards, the doe's fawn, seemingly fearful of the buck, followed dutifully in the breeding pair's path. At that moment, the doe's yearling, a 120-pound doe, crossed the faint trace that was once a logging trail. It was returning toward the browse area favored by its mother after drinking water from the beaver pond.

Ten minutes later, six grizzled wolves (an alpha female leading an alpha male and four grown pups), filing rapidly south along the old logging trail, abruptly halted and began sniffing the scent-laden tracks of the yearling doe, their tails wagging with obvious excitement. Shortly, the alpha male trailed by the four pups began a wide, downwind circling movement, their destination the southern, downwind terminus of the whitetail browse area.

About ten minutes later, the alpha female took stealthily to the trail of the yearling doe. Upon spotting it feeding 100 yards east of the logging trail, the wolf began a slow, cautious stalk, moving silently toward the deer only while it was noisily nipping browse, it's head hidden by intervening foliage. Upon inching toward a windfall about forty yards from its prey, the deer suddenly raised its head and stared back toward the wolf, its tail rising, white tail and rump hairs slowly becoming fully erect and glowing white. Realizing further stalking would be fruitless, the wolf sprang with all possible speed toward the deer. The yearling whirled and bounded straight away, heading east toward the downwind location of the five wolves now waiting in ambush. Upon hearing the snapping brush and staccato hoofbeats of the rapidly approaching deer, they began to adjusts their positions, moving south about 20 yards and fanning out, forming the deadly semicircle that would snap shut on the hard-pressed deer the moment it entered the trap.

As is often the case, however, the desperate deer, 10-mph faster than its pursuer, was rapidly increasing its lead. The moment it gained a safe distance, about 100 yards, the deer suddenly veered south, scrambling up a steep and treacherous slope some 80 yards short of the ambush site. Though briefly visible, the ambushers made no move toward the fleeing deer or its pursuer. About five minutes later the alpha female, panting heavily, rejoined the pack and the six wolves returned to the logging trail where they resumed their rapid pace south.

Meanwhile, the moment the first sounds of the bounding deer were heard, the adult doe, dominant buck and fawn moved quickly into a dense patch of osiers where they remained frozen as the yearling doe and wolf rushed past. About 30 minutes later, the doe and fawn resumed feeding and the buck resumed restlessly following the doe.

Over the past five years, I have watched similar scenes unfold many times. I have never witnessed these wolves hunting whitetails in any other manner. I therefore believe it is their primary method of hunting whitetails, if not their exclusive method. Though I cannot be certain this method is used by all wolves in this region, judging by wolf tracks I have discovered elsewhere, I believe it is. Only twice have I witnessed successful conclusions (for wolves), fawns taken both times. Nonetheless, considering the usual good health and vigor of these wolves, and the number of their kill sites I have discovered, it is obvious to me this hunting method is successful often enough.

Observations of wolf hunts, and tracks made by wolves while hunting whitetails, have been fountainheads for answers to questions concerning whitetail hunting by humans and tactics used by whitetails to avoid hunting humans, providing answers to mysteries that had vexed me more than twenty years. To illustrate the value of observations of wolves in the act of hunting, consider what can be gleaned from the above account.

First, consider the actions of the adult doe, dominant buck and fawn. From the outset, these deer obviously did not consider themselves in serious danger. The bounding deer was the intended prey of the wolf, not them. This being the case, it was unnecessary to flee. All they had to do is move aside and freeze in cover, avoiding discovery and possible threat. Thus secure, they did not panic upon spotting their most dreaded enemy. They wisely remained frozen for some time. Well after the pursuing wolf returned to the pack and the pack subsequently abandoned the area, these three deer remained frozen. After giving the wolves adequate time to clear the area, they resumed feeding, not displaying the least hint of nervousness.

This very same avoidance tactic is used successfully by all classes of whitetails in two of three short-range encounters (40–100 yards) with hunting humans. Whitetails characteristically use this tactic when it is obvious to them they are not intended prey and the predator or man is not moving directly toward them, inadvertently or not. Whitetails determine whether or not they are intended prey by noting (via sight, sounds and/or airborne odors) the behavior (hunting behavior or a lack of hunting behavior) of a potentially dangerous predator or man. This characteristic assessment of behavior generally begins while the predator or man is yet 100–200 yards away. Behavior that indicates to a whitetail it is an intended prey includes the following: 1) a sudden nearby halt (discovery behavior) followed by freezing or hiding, 2) stalking, attempting to move toward a deer (or its vicinity) without being detected, 3) frequent stopping to peer about, listen and sniff and inspect tracks, 4) staring toward the deer (whether the deer is actually seen or not) and 5) changing course (turning from a trail, for example) toward the deer.

All of these actions, almost continuously displayed, are characteristic of humans who hunt on foot, still-hunters a prime example.

Freezing in cover has a number of important benefits. First, it enables whitetails to avoid discovery and serious threat in two of three short-range encounters with potentially dangerous predators or man. Second, by making it unnecessary to flee with great speed every time a potentially dangerous predator or man is identified nearby, it enables whitetails to conserve energy; thus keeping their bodies fully charged for the moment when all possible speed is truly necessary. Third, it greatly reduces the need to significantly interrupt normal habits and behavior, enabling whitetails to live fairly serene and normal lives even where potentially dangerous predators and man are a frequent threat. Fourth, it enables whitetails to remain within their familiar home ranges, areas where they are most adept at identifying and avoiding danger.

Next, consider the actions of the yearling doe. Whether instinctive (genetically predisposed) or learned from older, more experienced deer, principally its mother, this whitetail did what all whitetails of yearling age or older do under similar circumstances. Upon realizing it was in grave danger, its first goal was to gain a safe distance as quickly as possible. Ordinarily, a yearling can outrun a wolf, but initially, while the wolf is fresh and very near, it can't make turns while fleeing. A pursuing wolf will cut corners and thus gain ground. To avoid giving a pursuing wolf any advantage, the pursued deer must run straight away until it is about 100 yards ahead. Once this is achieved, the deer can then safely change its course and begin making use of cover and terrain that discourages pursuit. In this case, the deer veered right and nimbly scaled a steep and treacherous slope. It probably would have been equally successful at ending the chase if it had veered left and bounded into the spruce bog. Once free to choose its escape route, a whitetail has the advantage, vaulting over obstacles and making use of terrain that will quickly slow a shorter-legged, less acrobatic pursuer such as a wolf or man.

Even if pursuit-discouraging cover or terrain had not been immediately available, the deer would have veered right or left upon gaining a 100-yard lead. This is especially characteristic of whitetails that live among wolves. Whether pursued by a fleet wolf or a plodding human (or driven by a skirmish line of humans), a yearling or adult whitetail expects an ambush ahead. As quickly as possible, therefore, it will avoid being pushed far in any one direction by wolf or man, especially downwind, a direction in which it cannot smell hidden danger. As soon as it is safe to turn, it will begin swinging into the wind, thereafter able to use its keen nose to identify and avoid hidden danger safe distances ahead.

Though wolves have long been absent from the ranges of whitetails in the Continental U.S., they were the principle predators of whitetails eons before man nearly eradicated them a century or so ago. Via thousands of years of selective cropping, deer most vulnerable to wolf ambushing were largely weeded out. When man became the whitetail's principle predator, whitetails everywhere were well prepared to deal with human ambushes. Though they faltered when human ambushers began climbing into trees, they are now about as adept at identifying and avoiding hunters in trees as hunters moving on foot on the ground.

Finally, consider the actions of the wolves. Judging by what I have often seen, wolves seem to have specific criteria in mind when selecting a whitetail prey. They seem careful to avoid wasting energy on deer they cannot catch. How they decide which deer can be caught and which cannot is yet somewhat of a mystery, but they seem capable of doing it via trail scent alone. While cruising in search of vulnerable prey, wolves hardly give many fresh trails of whitetails (notably adult deer) a passing sniff, likely recognizing them as trails of deer that cannot be caught, perhaps learned via previous attempts. This would explain, in part, why wolves sometimes continue past deer they can plainly see without displaying the least bit of interest, and why certain whitetails stand or lie boldly exposed as disinterested wolves trot past. Certainly, however, the behavior of the wolves plays a major role in determining how whitetails respond to them. While wolves (or human hunters) are not displaying hunting behavior and are moving steadily past at a safe distance, whitetails invariably show little or no alarm.

Some deer tracks draw considerable attention from wolves, and obvious excitement. Such tracks are sniffed repeatedly, the wolves often staring long moments in the direction taken by the deer, seemingly considering hunting strategies and weighing odds for success. Cover and terrain might be a predisposing factor, wolves being at an advantage in some areas and at a disadvantage in others. I tend to believe certain scents are a major deciding factor, scents that distinguish less fleet deer, fawns and deer slowed by wounds, starvation, age, disease or parasites. In my study area, fawns, wounded deer, starving deer (in winter yards) or bucks nearing age seven do not long escape being being tested (hunted) by wolves. A wolfpack's decision to hunt or ignore a certain deer is made by the alpha male or female, perhaps both. While cruising, gangly-legged juveniles seem anxious to take to every fresh deer trail, but if they become too interested in scents of a trail their parents ignore, they are soon left behind, obliged to scurry to rejoin the pack.

Less mysterious is the manner in which wolves orchestrate their hunts. It's probably simply a matter of scents, the driving wolf approaching the selected prey via trail scent and the ambushing wolves positioning themselves at the proper location downwind by centering themselves on the prey's airborne scents.

On the surface it might appear wolves have nothing new to teach us about hunting whitetails. After all, the downwind drive is one of our most popular hunting methods, and no doubt about it, drives account for an enormous number of whitetails taken by human hunters each fall. Typically, however, few older bucks are taken by humans making drives. Whereas most hunters who use this hunting method are quick to believe there can't be many older bucks in the areas they hunt, if any, this is hardly ever true. Older bucks rarely fall prey to human drives simply because they are very adept at avoiding ambushers (standers). Generally, experienced adult bucks either abandon areas to be driven well before drives begin, they outflank advancing skirmish lines of drivers or they freeze in dense cover as unwitting drivers march steadily past.

Every single adult buck not harvested by human hunters in my hunting region is eventually caught and eaten by wolves. In this region bucks rarely survive beyond age 6-1/2, if that. Obviously, though our hunting methods may be similar, wolves know how to regularly take the largest of bucks, and we don't, or can't.

One basic reason is, we're not wolves. We do not have the advantage a wolf-like nose, the origin of the extraordinary sensitivity of a Bloodhound's nose. We cannot identify and pinpoint locations of deer and position ourselves downwind via airborne scents. We don't have the advantage of wolf-like ears, the origin of the waterfowl retriever's ears that can hear ducks approaching long before the hunter can hear or see them. We cannot identify and pinpoint locations of deer via hearing unless they are very near. We don't have the advantage of wolf-like eyes, 100-times more sensitive than our eyes in subdued light and capable of spotting the least motion in heavy cover. We cannot spot deer unless they are situated in areas where they can easily spot us. We don't have the advantage of wolf-like paws, capable of carrying a wolf silently over practically any surface. Having large, clumsy feet made insensitive to what we step on by huge, unyielding boots, we cannot move far in typical whitetail habitat without making sounds easily heard and identified by whitetails 100–200 yards or more away. We don't have the advantage of wolf-like fur, whisper-quiet and very difficult to spot in forest cover. The clothing we are obliged to wear, intended to make us highly visible to other hunters and provide protection from inclement weather, makes it very easy for whitetails to identify us via sight and hearing at safe ranges. We don't have the advantage of a wolf-like body, capable of slipping with ease through deer-sized openings in dense forest cover. Being upright, twice as tall as a whitetail, and having wide, square shoulders, we cannot avoid making the telltale sounds that come from brushing against or pushing through trailside branches and foliage. We don't have the advantage of wolf-like speed. We cannot run fast enough or far enough to force whitetails to flee with reckless abandon into the clutches of waiting ambushers. We're pretty sorry wolves. Unfortunately, wherever we hunt, whitetails treat us as if we are wolves.

During the process of developing Johnny-on-the-spot buck hunting, close-range encounters with wolves became notably more and more common. This may simply be a matter of the wolves becoming increasingly tame in my presence, or it may be a measure of the effectiveness of Johnny-on-the-spot buck hunting. Being more regularly close to deer logically means I will more regularly be close to wolves. However, I favor another notion, whimsical as it may be. These wolves have always approached from downwind, indicating they go out of their way to visit me upon identifying my airborne odors. They have never in all our meetings displayed the least hint of hostile behavior, suggesting they do not consider me an intruder, competitor or prey. Nor have they have ever appeared shy about showing me how they hunt whitetails. Though I can't begin to fathom what may be going through their minds during our close encounters, it is not difficult to imagine they may actually be trying to teach me how to be a better whitetail hunter, sorry wolf that I am. If this is true, these days, I think these wolves depart feeling just a bit proud of themselves.

The wolf has much to teach us.

Though it is physically impossible for humans to hunt exactly like wolves, at least three hunting practices that contribute greatly to the hunting success of wolves can be used by human hunters. When used by human hunters, they loose some of their effectiveness, but they work well enough to put skilled hunters within 100 yards of at least one adult buck during practically every half-day of hunting. The three adoptable wolf hunting practices are as follows:

1. Key on Vulnerable Deer

A vulnerable buck—passing within easy shooting range

Wolves key only on deer that are vulnerable for one reason or another. To wolves, "vulnerable" means 1) the intended prey cannot run faster than a wolf (adult whitetails are ordinarily 10 mph faster), the deer being young or weakened or slowed by deep snow and thus easily caught or steered toward an ambush, or 2) the deer is currently located in an area where cover and/or terrain will make it especially difficult for a selected prey to avoid ambush.

Keying on vulnerable bucks is

a principle element of Johnny-on-the-spot buck hunting. To the Johnny-on-the-spot buck hunter, however, the word "vulnerable" has one different meaning and one similar meaning. The different meaning is attributable to the one advantage human hunters have over wolves—deadly, long-range weaponry. Modern archery equipment and firearms enable human hunters to dispatch deer at ranges of 30–100 yards or more. In typical whitetail habit, open shoots (no intervening obstacles) are uncommon beyond 50 yards. Archery equipment is most deadly at a range of 10–30 yards. To the Johnny-on-the-spot buck hunter, then, "vulnerable" means 1) the intended prey is likely to pass within 10–50 yards or 2) an intended prey is currently located in an area where cover and/or terrain will make it especially difficult for the intended prey to avoid an ambush.

2. Scout Daily

Wolves scout daily, searching for and keying on very fresh signs of unalarmed (unsuspecting) deer only, actually, fresh trail scents only. Very fresh deer signs are indisputable evidence a potential victim is near. Wolves never waste time or energy hunting in areas devoid of vulnerable prey. They never set up a drive, merely hoping a deer is located between the driver and ambushers (standers). Though not successful every time they begin a hunt, because wolves always key on very fresh deer signs only, *they are always in the right place at the right time.*

The manner in which these master predators scout daily is also vital to their hunting success. Their scouting is very different from their hunting. While scouting, they cruise rapidly (walking) along specific routes, moving steadily, pausing infrequently and then very briefly, rarely straying off-trail until they have discovered the scents of a vulnerable prey.

To key on fresh signs only, the hunter must scout daily.

Wolf cruise routes are paths that lend to rapid movements throughout enormous hunting ranges (100 square-miles or more). Favorite cruise routes are old logging trails, well-worn deer trails, uncluttered river banks (river ice in winter) and such. These routes course through whitetail home ranges, crossing countless trails and sites frequented by whitetails.

Cruise routes enable wolves to quickly and regularly assess trail scents of every deer within their ranges without significantly alarming potential prey. As long as wolves remain on their established cruise routes and do not display hunting behavior, whitetails will do little more than move aside, if necessary, and freeze in cover as their seemingly disinterested enemies move steadily past. Accustomed to the harmlessness of wolves that are merely cruising, some adult deer will freeze boldly in the open as they pass, the wolves giving them little more than a sidelong glance, if that. This very productive means of scouting insures intended prey will be near when the decision is made to begin a hunt.

The Johnny-on-the-spot buck hunter scouts like a wolf: scouting daily along a few pre-chosen paths coursing across trails or about sites frequented by one or more adult bucks, the hunter avoiding any display of hunting behavior and ignoring all but very fresh deer signs made by adult bucks.

3. Quickly Hunt Vulnerable Deer

Unlike human hunters, wolves do not take note of a fresh deer trail and return to hunt the deer that made that trail days or weeks later. They do not ignore fresh signs of a vulnerable prey because they are committed to hunting elsewhere. Upon discovering the fresh trail of a vulnerable deer, they hunt that deer right now, while it is yet near and vulnerable.

The portable stool makes it possible to key quickly on vulnerable bucks.

Keying quickly on fresh signs of adult bucks is a primary reason Johnny-on-the-spot buck hunting is so effective. Lacking the necessary stealth and speed, this wolf-like hunting practice is modified in a way that enables hulking, clumsy creatures such you or me to become very difficult for the most wary of bucks to identify, and, if identified, to appear harmless. Upon discovering the fresh signs of a buck, the hunter moves stealthily to a downwind site likely to be in the path of the quarry, right now, later that day, or at the latest, before first light the next morning. There, seated on a portable stool and hidden by natural, unaltered cover, the motionless hunter quietly waits until the unsuspecting quarry appears, not stirring until about 11 AM or sunset.

Effectiveness

Gray wolves can pinpoint exact locations of unseen whitetails located

100 yards or more away and then stalk to within 40 yards of them without being identified, enabling wolves to feast on venison almost every day they are inclined to hunt whitetails. Unless quarries can actually be seen, human hunters cannot pinpoint exact locations of whitetails located 100 yards or more away and rarely can human hunters stalk to within 40 yards of whitetails without being identified. The best human hunters can do is pinpoint *likely* locations of whitetails, plus or minus 100 yards or so, and then move stealthily to downwind or crosswind stand sites situated within 10–50 yards of routes *likely* to be taken by deer moving away from predicted current locations.

For human hunters, then, hunting success hinges on the word "likely." In this case "likely" means "more apt to be in the area predicted than not," or "more apt to use the route predicted than not." The word "likely," of course, is a relative term, expressible in terms of percentages or odds. Johnny-on-the-spot buck hunting is the most effective means I know for keying on sites where adult bucks are likely to pass within 10–50 yards, but even under the most favorable circumstances, adult bucks do not pass within 10–50 yards during every half-day of hunting; only a percentage of them. Adding to the percentage of unproductive hunting time attributable to the fact that adult bucks are not ordinarily 100% predictable. Moreover, unfavorable circumstances commonly materialize in consequence of factors not attributable to the hunter. More often than not, however, the hunter, or a human failing, is at fault.

Whereas the Johnny-on-the-spot approach cannot provide opportunities to harvest one or more adult bucks during *every* half-day of hunting, it can put the hunter within 100 yards of one or more adult bucks during at least nine of ten half-days of hunting. Such nearness is a desirable advantage, but when the quarry is an adult buck keenly aware of being hunted, such nearness can also be a curse. It pits the easily-lulled sensory perceptions, alertness, camouflage, coolness under pressure, judgment, patience and stealth of a two-day-per-year, urban-dwelling human against the sensory perceptions, camouflage, coolness under pressure, judgment, patience and stealth of an extra-alert deer that has successfully avoided mortal danger during as many days as the average human hunter could hunt in 10–25 lifetimes. Adult bucks are not infallible, but the average hunter's ability to identify an adult buck 100 yards away cannot begin to match an adult buck's ability to identify a hunter 100 yards away, and the average hunter's ability to avoid discovery by an adult buck 100 yards away cannot begin to match an adult buck's ability to avoid discovery by a hunter 100 yards away. In most cases the human hunter will remain totally unaware of being approached, studied and avoided by an adult buck. Perseverance, *attention to detail* and unrelenting caution, hallmarks of the successful Johnny-on-the-spot buck hunter, will occasionally tip the scale in favor of the hunter, and adult bucks will occasionally make fatal errors, either on their own or as a result of skillful actions on the part of the hunter. But only, of course, during a percentage of half-days of hunting.

Though it is possible to predict with surprising accuracy and regularity an adult buck's current location, its next destination and the 100–200 yard-wide lane it will use to get from one to the other, predicting the exact paths it will use is wholly another matter. The difficulty is attributable to an adult buck's characteristically cunning (intelligent) use of trails. Whatever its destination, and whatever direction it approaches from, an adult buck will generally have a dozen or more different ways (routes) to get there. While hunting is in progress, not only will adult bucks make use of trails that provide the greatest security, trails coursing through dense cover and/or located downwind of a known or likely location of hunters, but older bucks, especially, will seldom use the same trails twice in a row—both very effective means of foiling ambushers. Moreover, during hunting seasons, older bucks, especially, will travel off-trail up to 50% of the time. All this makes it impossible to predict with 10–50 yard precision the paths of adult bucks during every half-day of hunting. Nonetheless, the hunter must constantly strive for such precision. This requirement is the only way to significantly improve buck hunting success. *You can't take 'em if you don't get within 10–50 yards.* About 90% of all bucks taken by my hunting partners and me since adopting the Johnny-on-the-spot approach were traveling toward predicted destinations along established deer trails.

By no means does this mean buck hunting success is merely a matter of luck. If the hunter recognizes information provided by deer signs, understands whitetail habits and knows the locations of key whitetail home range elements such as feeding and bedding areas, the word "likely" means "correct up to 90% of the time," i.e., "within 100 yards during nine of ten half-days of hunting."

To illustrate how it works, consider words I have often uttered over the past twenty-some years: "Judging by the length of these tracks (or droppings) and their freshness, the deer that made these tracks is a 3-1/2 to 6-1/2 year-old buck and it is not far away. Whitetails are currently feeding. This buck headed toward a currently-favored feeding area 200 yards west of here. It is likely, therefore, this buck is now 200 yards or so west of here."

When you can identity and determine the approximate whereabouts of a whitetail in this fashion, you will rarely be wrong. If you can then get to a downwind or crosswind perimeter of that buck's current location without its knowledge, and if you can then sit quietly on a stool, hidden by natural, unaltered cover within easy shooting range of signs made by that buck during the previous 6–24 hours, your odds for taking that buck will be as favorable as they can be for taking any deer, including a fawn or yearling. Some hunters may choose to call it "luck," but it's not luck. Johnny-on-the-spot buck hunting is a means of making aces and kings out of deer signs and whitetail savvy, providing the hunter with the best of odds at all times.

Adult bucks, especially dominant bucks, have been my exclusive quarries since 1970. Since adopting the Johnny-on-the-spot approach, I've taken one dominant buck during the first half-day of a hunting season, but it generally takes me eight or more half-days to finally zero in on the right place at the right time. My less-fussy sons and daughters, not having the luxury of being able to hunt up to sixteen days in a row, regularly take 2-1/2 year-old bucks within four half-days of hunting.

At this moment, the largest buck I've ever had the opportunity to hunt is lying within its mountaintop bedding area, its great antlers yet half-grown. Having studied this buck's habits and home range very thoroughly, I find it difficult to believe it will not be standing or moving slowly 10-50 yards away within eight half-days of hunting this coming fall (nearly fifty years of whitetail hunting has tempered my incurable optimism somewhat, so I'm also prepared to endure thirty-two half-days of sitting if I must). Unless I discover the opportunity to use our "gentle nudge" hunting method (100% effective thus far) or unless I run out of time and decide to use our "cover-all-bases" hunting method (67% effective thus far), the Johnny-on-the-spot approach is the only hunting method I dare use while hunting such a buck. No other method can be as trusted to keep such a buck from altering its habits or abandoning its range. No other method could put me as near this buck and as often over as long a period of time. These are the reasons my six hunting partners and I are dedicated Johnny-on-the-spot buck hunters. These are the reasons my hunting partners and I quickly harvest our self-imposed limit of 3-4 adult bucks per season in a region where very few adult bucks are taken by other hunters. These are the reasons we each enjoy watching 20-40 non-quarries within fifty yards per hunting season. Using traditional hunting methods, only about one in thirty hunters takes an adult buck per hunting season. The Johnny-on-the-spot buck hunting method can provide one or more opportunities to harvest one or more adult bucks per hunting season.

Buck hunting doesn't get any better than that.

Step 1: Pre-Season Scouting

During the five hunting seasons my partners and I used our most productive of buck hunting methods—the "Johnny-on-the-spot" and "cover-all-bases" approaches, plus the "gentle nudge"—few of the adult bucks we hunted were taken on opening morning. One-half to two thirds were taken on the second, third or fourth day (at the third-to-eighth stand site used). Two dominant bucks did not make a fatal mistake until the fifteenth and sixteenth days. When hunting adult bucks only, therefore, though there's nothing wrong with attempting to take a certain buck on opening morning, it's foolish to plan and prepare no further; foolish to risk hunting success on one stand site; foolish to believe (or hope) an intended quarry will appear sooner or later, patience the key to success.

Because the hunter can expect to be successful during only a small percentage of opening mornings and because after opening morning adult bucks can be expected to change the trails and areas they will use, as often as necessary, the hunter must begin each hunting season prepared to closely follow an intended quarry, changing stand sites as often as necessary. To accomplish this feat, like wolves, the hunter must scout daily for signs made by the quarry during the previous 6–24 hours and quickly key on them. Only this can keep the hunter in *the right places at the right times*, half-day after half-day.

To know where to scout while hunting and to recognize *right places at right times*, the hunter must understand deer signs, understand whitetail habits, understand factors that alter the timing of whitetail movements, be familiar with trails and sites currently frequented by the quarry, especially bedding and feeding areas, and be familiar with trails and sites likely to be frequented by the buck after the hunting season begins.

Such knowledge will regularly put the hunter within 100 yards of adult bucks, but in the end, two hunting skills are needed to close the range to the necessary 10–50 yards: stealth and the ability to appear harmless.

In buck hunting, stealth is the ability to avoid being seen, heard or smelled by whitetails located within 200 yards. Such stealth requires a great deal of concentration. The way most hunters hunt, adequate stealth is impossible to sustain more than a few minutes at a time, lapses typically occurring at worst possible moments (grist for countless tales about big bucks that got away). The reason is, while walking in the sort of cover whitetails live in, tall, upright humans cannot concentrate on stealth and spotting a deer at the same time. To avoid revealing sounds such as those made when branches, foliage and other objects are stepped on or pushed aside, the hunter's eyes must be cast downward, eyes assessing the forest floor immediately ahead before each step is taken. To spot a deer, the hunter's eyes must be cast toward the horizon, focussing on everything deer-tall from left to right, 50–100 yards ahead. The hunter's eyes cannot be pointed at both places at the same time.

To insure stealth will be adequate when adequate stealth is most needed, rather than scan surroundings in search of deer, while mid-hunt scouting or approaching stand sites while in areas in which it is likely an adult buck is less than 200 yards away, the hunter must concentrate on stealth only—

watch each step. Adequate stealth begins with knowing where and when a buck is likely to be within 200 yards; knowing where and when to utilize effective screening cover, where and when to avoid stepping on or pushing through branches and foliage that may make easily heard sounds and where and when to be downwind.

Within a relatively short period of time most whitetail hunters come to realize they cannot be stealthy and spot deer at the same time. In an attempt to solve this vexing problem, most adopt a routine erroneously referred to as "still-hunting"—cautiously moving short distances and halting often to peer about and listen. Typically anxious to spot a deer, such hunters can't wait to get to places where they imagine they will spot a deer, the next bend in the trail or the top of the next rise, for example. Peering about and listening soon begins well before the need to move cautiously has ended. Inevitably, peering about becomes a full-time activity, stealth largely forgotten. Those who call themselves "still-hunters" are thus the easiest of all hunters for whitetails to identify at safe ranges (100–200 yards), and the easiest to avoid.

As far as whitetails are concerned, such hunters also exhibit the most dangerous kind of behavior. Whether identified via sight, hearing or smell, the actions of a human moving furtively and halting often to peer about and listen intently are exactly like those of any large predator stalking a deer. If a human displaying such behavior is discovered within 100 yards, a super-wary adult buck is likely to believe it is the selected prey, in which case it will abandon its range or become completely nocturnal, making it impossible to hunt.

There are only two ways to avoid the ruinous consequences of moving furtively on foot and stopping often to peer about and listen: 1) don't get caught—concentrate wholly on avoiding identification by using adequate stealth within 200 yards of an adult buck—or 2) don't display hunting behavior, at least not while within 200 yards of an adult buck.

To properly set the stage for successful Johnny-on-the-spot buck hunting, the hunter needs to know the following: 1) locations of 2–3 suitable quarries, 2) locations of buck inhabited areas to scout while hunting and how to get to them without alerting or alarming quarries, 3) locations of a good number of likely ground-level stand sites and how to get to them without alerting or alarming quarries and 4) the location of a prime stand site for opening morning. To satisfy these vital needs, the hunter must scout before the hunting season begins.

A relatively small percentage of whitetail hunters scout before hunting. Many reasons are given: *it's a waste of time*, *I don't have enough time* and *I can't afford it* among the most popular. Few admit the real reason: *I don't know enough about deer signs to make scouting worthwhile.* Most who must scout, namely stand hunters, generally suffer the same shortcoming. The majority of stand sites I've inspected over the past 25 years were obviously selected for two reasons: 1) the nearby deer trail appeared well-used and 2) deer can be seen approaching at a great distance. Unfortunately, such reasons severely limit any chance of taking an adult buck.

Whatever your reason might be for not scouting, or not scouting adequately, if you want to enjoy the extraordinary success of Johnny-on-the-spot buck hunting, the time has come to say, "Yes Dear, I know I spend too much time deer hunting, but if I'm going to get that big buck this year, I've got to get out there and scout." You might even add, "Why don't you come along. I think you'll enjoy it. We'll picnic at a special spot I know, pick berries, and afterwards, I'll take you out for dinner."

To ease you into beginning this seemingly onerous task, to make you as effective a scouter as I am, there are four things you should know about scouting in preparation for Johnny-on-the-spot buck hunting.

First, it's a lot easier than you might imagine. Though there are eight kinds of deer signs—tracks, trails, droppings, beds, antler rubs, ground scrapes, evidences of feeding and evidences of watering—and enough variations of each to add up to more than 200 different deer signs, you don't need to find and understand all of them to do a first-class job of scouting. In fact, if you know little more than how to distinguish the tracks and droppings of adult bucks from the tracks and droppings of other deer, if you understand antler rubs and if you recognize obvious signs of browsing, you know enough to take one or more braggin'-sized bucks every hunting season.

What about ground scrapes? Ignore them. That's right, ignore them. There are plenty of experts around who will vigorously argue otherwise, but you can easily prove for yourself that you will be a much more successful buck hunter if you do not deliberately hunt near buck ground scrapes, real or otherwise, and if you do not use buck lures of any kind.

Second, while scouting, you don't need to see bucks, only signs made by bucks. In fact, if you see a buck, you should ignore it. Don't allow its location or whatever it is doing to influence your planning.

Third, all you really have to locate are the areas where adult bucks spend more than 90% of their time during any one day of hunting, namely, bedding and feeding areas. If you use the Johnny-on-the-spot approach and key exclusively on buck bedding and feeding areas, you will see many times more unsuspecting adult bucks within fifty yards than when hunting elsewhere, using any other hunting method.

Fourth, Johnny-on-the-spot buck hunting does not require a tedious, days-long, learn-everything kind of scouting. It can be divided into parts, each part relatively quick and easy. I traditionally begin with a fast-moving, far-ranging kind of scouting, used to locate suitable quarries and their approximate ranges only (it is unnecessary to know the exact boundaries of buck ranges)—*quarry scouting*. In fall I follow up with a zeroing-in kind of scouting, used to locate trails and sites frequented by individual bucks—*range element scouting*. Because it is only necessary to scout two or three buck ranges, commit to only one stand site (for opening morning) and because stand sites are not altered in any way, this scouting is far less taxing and far less time consuming than when preparing for conventional tree stand hunting. If you are accustomed to tree stand hunting, this scouting will seem "too easy." Finally, there's the cautious, conservative, daily scouting used to locate new stand sites while hunting—*mid-hunt scouting*. This. too, can be kept very simple, often little more than a matter of keeping an eye peeled for fresh deer signs while traveling to and from stand sites. *Cold scouting*, a slower and more thorough kind of scouting is generally only necessary when preparing to hunt a new and unfamiliar hunting area.

There now, feel better?

Locating 2–3 Suitable Quarries

Because Johnny-on-the-spot buck hunting will put the hunter within 100 yards of a desirable buck twice daily, sooner or later the two must meet. If all goes well for the hunter, that will be the end of the hunt. If all goes well for the buck (the odds favor the buck), that will also be the end of the hunt. The buck will raise its tail (flaring white hairs of its tail and rump reflecting great alarm), whirl and flee, bounding or trotting, perhaps snorting a time or two. Within a jump or two, the buck will disappear from sight. It will be 100 yards away in a matter of 5–6 seconds. The buck will not rest until it is safe from any repeat of so fearsome a blunder. No longer able to trust its senses to protect it from dangerous encounters with human hunters, the buck will bed at a distant, well-hidden site and not move during daylight hours, or it will flee to a place of proven security, near or far off-range, some nearly impenetrable swamp, a steep and treacherous slope or an area surrounded by fences or signs that mysteriously stop human pursuit. Characteristically, the buck's fear will not abate for a period of 5–10 days, longer if sounds of human hunters continue to echo from is home or breeding range. Typically, the anguished hunter will sit near trails and sites previously frequented by the buck until the sun drops from sight on the final day of hunting. This is almost always a waste of time. When an adult buck raises it tail and bounds away, it's best to forget that buck and move on to another quarry. Because the odds always favor an adult buck, the hunter who intends to harvest an adult buck should never begin a hunting season prepared to hunt less than two adult bucks. Three is better.

If it wasn't for the profound manner in which adult bucks respond to the near presence of humans, the most ideal time to scout would be the day before the opener, thus reducing as much as possible the likelihood an intended quarry will be using different trails and different sites on opening morning. To accomplish all that must be accomplished, to provide the best odds for taking an adult buck, however, the hunter must be completely free to stomp anywhere without regard for consequences. At least once per year, the hunter must be free to assess just-made tracks, droppings and beds of adult bucks wherever they are. At least once per year, the hunter must be free to bust in on feeding and bedding deer. At least once per year, therefore, bucks must be deliberately and thoroughly spooked, and 2–3 weeks before the opener is the time to do it.

Why once per year at this time? The habits of adult bucks (lesser, non-breeding adult bucks and dominant breeding bucks) may be similar from year-to-year, and many buck ground scrapes will be at the exact same locations from year to year (only significant for hunting during the 2–3 weeks before breeding begins), but each adult buck and each successor of adult bucks that died during the previous fall or winter will be different enough each fall to require at least one thorough scouting annually. At least once each year, the hunter must get an idea (it doesn't have to be perfect) of how many adult bucks there are in the area to be hunted and how big they are. At least once per year the hunter must know exactly where they bed, feed, water and travel (the trails they favor). It is impossible to get close to adult bucks (in their paths) half-day after half-day without knowing such things. You have to be sure. While engaged in the pursuit of all this vital knowledge, many or all adult bucks will decide it is prudent to temporarily abandon their ranges and/or become completely nocturnal. Pre-season scouting should therefore be completed at least 2–3 weeks before hunting begins—early enough to insure quarries will have fully recovered from the shock of discovering a dreaded human poking around favorite (normally secure) trails and range areas; late enough to insure quarries will not have made great changes in range utilization before the opener. Scouting 2-3 weeks early is not an ideal compromise, but if an adult buck is the intended quarry, it's the only compromise.

This does not mean the hunter should not scout at other times. In fact, it's a good idea. Not only will scouting at other times shorten the list of what must be accomplished 2–3 weeks before the opener, but it will enable the hunter to concentrate only on areas likely to be frequented by bucks during the hunting season. A lot of what must be done—locating suitable quarries and their bedding areas, watering spots and many of their feeding areas—can be accomplished any time from snow-melt in early spring (1–2 weeks after whitetails disperse from wintering areas, giving deer adequate time to create signs throughout their newly established or reestablished home ranges) until 2–3 weeks before a hunting season begins and anytime from 1–2 weeks after a hunting season ends (giving deer adequate time to return to normal ranges and begin creating signs at previously frequented trails and sites) until whitetails migrate to wintering areas in late December.

Pre-season scouting is not particularly productive while whitetails are in winter quarters. From late December until snow-melt in early spring, most whitetails congregate in areas that provide adequate foods and superior cover from winter winds and storms, commonly heavily forested or brushy wet lowlands, habitable only after water is frozen. Most are located within a few miles of summer home ranges but some are as far as thirty miles away. During mid and late winter, therefore, few, if any, fresh signs will be found in previously established home ranges—areas where whitetails are normally located during hunting seasons. If not covered by snow, buck antler rubs and ground scrapes will be visible, but their usefulness for planning future hunts will be questionable. The bucks that made them may not have survived the previous hunting season, and if they did, they may not survive the winter. Few bucks 6-1/2 years of age survive to see another spring. If a buck fails to survive hunting or winter, it may take up to two years before another buck will claim its range. If the new buck is a two-year-old establishing its first individual home range, often the case, it will not adopt an older buck's entire range—only one-third to one-half of it. Moreover, whatever the age of the succeeding buck, with the exception of most scrape sites, it will not necessarily frequent the same trails and sites, including the previous buck's bedding area. For that matter, if a previous bedding area was visited too often by a human hunter, a returning buck is very likely to establish a new bedding area some distance away.

Hunters who scout in midwinter are also vulnerable to making a classic error. Upon discovering a whitetail wintering area, characteristically loaded with fresh deer signs, the hunter is likely to believe a hunting Shangri-la has been found. Following considerable pre-season dreaming, planning and preparation, the hunter will invariably end up wondering how in the world an area so loaded with deer signs could end up so completely devoid of deer. Generally, hunting plans and preparations based on midwinter scouting are not nearly as fruitful as hunting plans and preparations based on scouting during any other period of the year.

Though certainly not the only course to follow, besides scouting 2–3 weeks before the opener, I favor scouting shortly after snow-melt in early spring.

Each spring, my hunting partners and I anxiously await the day when the sun has at last melted away the hip-deep snow that almost always blankets our deer country in late winter. When one of several long-distance telephone calls finally yields the answer, "There are only a few patches of snow left in the woods and deer are feeding along roadsides," we drop everything and head north, taking advantage of the small window of time between snow-melt and the emergence of new leaves and hordes of mosquitoes and woodticks. Whitetails gratefully depart from their browse-depleted wintering areas a week or two earlier, quickly establishing or reestablishing their individual home ranges. At this time it is especially easy to find deer signs that identify adult bucks and the areas in which they live.

Cattle-type mineral blocks provided in spring increase antler size up to 20%.

As is our custom, we begin our annual spring ritual by sledding antler-growth-enhancing, cattle-type mineral blocks to buck bedding areas in half of my study area (another research project in progress). We then split up and head to favorite hunting areas, cruising widely in search of the fresh signs that will kindle summer-long dreams featuring big bucks—potent incentives for extra thoroughness while preparing for fall hunting.

Spring scouting cannot provide all of the information needed for fall hunting, but it has several notable advantages over scouting at other times of the year. Annual grasses and shrubs are absent or flattened by snow, making hiking much easier. Before new leaves form, deer trails are more visible than at any other time of the year, often clearly visible hundreds of yards away. Buck signs such as antler rubs and ground scrapes—signposts of previously established breeding ranges of dominant bucks, temporary ranges of displaced lesser bucks and bedding areas of adult bucks (marked by clusters of antler rubs)—are also visible over great distances, nearly as fresh and bright in appearance as the day they were made. The signs my hunting partners and I are most interested in finding at this time, fresh adult-buck-sized tracks and droppings, are also much easier to spot, tracks sharply defined in the soft, damp and turfless soil of early spring.

While scouting in spring, our number-one goal is to locate suitable numbers of suitable quarries (quarry scouting). Bucks 2-1/2 years of age are considered "acceptable," but only if we cannot find 6–8 or more older bucks. We generally limit our harvests to half of the 3-1/2 – 6-1/2 year-old bucks present in our hunting area. This not only provides us with all the venison we care to eat in a year, but it insures each and every hunting season will be characterized by that special anticipation and excitement that

Tracks of certain sizes reveal where adult bucks live.

Droppings of certain sizes are as revealing as tracks.

comes with hunting bucks with enormous antlers. Thus we take to our separate paths each spring, anxiously seeking answers to two burning questions: 1) did big bucks not taken during the previous fall survive winter (and peak wolf predation) and 2) did new adult bucks settle in the home ranges of bucks taken during the previous hunting season?

Fresh tracks and droppings provide the answers. Being 33–100% heavier than other deer and significantly larger in stature, adult bucks (not including yearling bucks) have measurably larger tracks and droppings than other deer. In Minnesota where I hunt, adult does and yearling bucks have tracks measuring about 4-1/2 inches from tip to dewclaw (two-thirds that for hoof only) and droppings that measure 1/2-inch in length, not including the nubbins at the ends (to accurately identify whitetails via dropping lengths, disregard the few larger or smaller droppings in any one grouping). Our 2-1/2 year-old bucks have tracks measuring about 5 inches in length, droppings, 3/8 inch in length. Our dream-maker bucks, 3-1/2 – 6-1/2 year-olds, have tracks measuring 5-1/2 – 6 inches in length and droppings measuring 3/4 – 1-1/4 inches (for scientifically-determined track and dropping measurements specific to your hunting area, plus detailed information regarding more than 200 other deer signs, see *Whitetail Hunter's Almanac, 4th Edition*).

One fresh 5-1/2-inch track or one fresh 3/4-inch dropping is all it takes to establish the fact that a certain big buck lives, and where (roughly). One fresh 6-inch track or one fresh 1-inch dropping and one fresh 5-inch track or one fresh 3/8-inch dropping in the same area is all it takes to establish the fact that two other adult bucks live in roughly the same area. Similar discoveries a mile away or on the opposite side of a series of beaver ponds, a large swamp, a wide, rushing stream, a wide opening or other natural range-separating topography establish the fact that other adult bucks of specific ages or sizes live in those areas as well. Come fall, it is almost certain the tracks and droppings of all of these bucks will be found in the same general areas. When it is time to begin our more demanding pre-hunt scouting in fall, each of us having 2-3 different quarries in mind, we know exactly where to begin, making our fall scouting time much more productive.

If you decide to delay quarry scouting until fall, there's nothing wrong with combining this scouting with range element scouting. It will probably take more time, however. Moving relatively fast, I can usually make a circuit of my favorite buck hunting areas and locate and identify all the big bucks I could possibly hunt in a year within a half-day of scouting in spring. In fall, it usually takes a full day, soil being firm or dry and loose, making tracks difficult to measure accurately. and ground cover being fully mature, making tracks and dropping difficult to spot. Following the third week of September, falling leaves add to the difficulty.

Fortunately for me, Jene likes to tag along when I scout, spring or fall. I have to admit, she is much better at spotting tracks and droppings in deep grasses and shrubs than I am. I'm better at spotting antler rubs. Though I can predict almost exactly where we will find a certain buck's tracks and droppings, Jene invariably spots them first, frequently finding it necessary to call me back to inspect tracks or droppings I had nearly stepped on a moment or two earlier.

When quarry scouting in fall, I generally begin in wet (damp) lowlands lush with grasses and shrubs, areas where mature trees are sparse or absent. Such areas are almost certain to be whitetail feeding areas, deer gorging on greens to accumulate fat stores for the coming winter. Within such areas I rarely fail to discover plenty of fresh deer tracks and droppings, including at least a few that positively identify one or more adult bucks. The soil being damp and soft, tracks are much easier to spot and measure than elsewhere. For the same reason, I also check creek and swamp crossings (established deer trails) and watering spots, especially those within or around perimeters of areas previously inhabited by adult bucks. It is difficult to gauge the age of tracks in soft soils or mud, but at this point, as long as the tracks were obviously made within the previous week, age is not as important as numbers and sizes (lengths). Whether found on a trail or off-trail, lots of buck-sized tracks, fresh and old, not only reveal the presence of an adult buck and the location of at least a portion of its home range, but they are indisputable evidence the trail or area is often used or visited (currently frequented) by an adult buck (determining why, to be explained later, is the essence of range element scouting).

Tracks may not be readily spotted or measured in areas that are dry or covered with lush ground cover or fallen leaves, but this does not mean I ignore such areas while scouting for big bucks. In such areas I keep my eyes peeled for deer droppings. Droppings can provide the exact same information provided by tracks. Whether found on a trail or off-trail, lots of buck-sized droppings, fresh and old, also reveal the presence of an adult buck, the location of at least a portion of its home range and a trail or area often used or visited (currently frequented) by that buck.

Up to this point, you have probably noticed I have not explained how to identify adult bucks via other common deer signs, notably beds, antler rubs and ground scrapes. There are several reasons.

Though bed-lengths provide the most accurate means of identifying buck classes, especially in spring or fall, beds of adult bucks are characteristically difficult to find. This is not merely because they are usually well hidden, but because, unlike adult does, yearlings and fawns, adult bucks prefer to bed in dense woody cover where ground cover is sparse; where there is little to create a lasting impression of a bedded buck's body.

Until nights become cool 2–3 weeks before breeding begins, the only relatively fresh antler rubs to be found are a few slender velvet rubs. Such rubs are usually located within or very near bedding areas of adult bucks, but they cannot reveal much about the relative sizes of the bucks that made them. Larger-diameter rubs that do identify yearlings, 2-1/2 year-olds and 3-1/2 – 6-1/2 year-olds and difficult-to-read ground scrapes do not appear until 2–3 weeks before breeding begins, long after many hunters, especially bowhunters, begin hunting whitetails. Rubs and scrapes made during the previous fall may be recognizable, but these do not guarantee the adult bucks that made them are still alive and in the area.

When scouting for signs of suitable quarries, then, tracks and droppings are all you really need. Nothing in the woods can make conclusions arrived at via scouting more accurate. In fact, tracks and droppings should be considered the mainstay of all scouting, being very reliable for identifying whitetails and their range elements and the most abundant of deer signs whatever the season.

Locating Mid-Hunt Scouting Areas and Approaches—

Range Element Scouting

My studies of whitetails and whitetail hunting have often made it necessary to write of subjects no one has ever written of before, at least not to my knowledge. Now and then, I must therefore create a new term and/or definition. The following definition of a whitetail range element, a term often used in this book and of particular importance to this subject, is an example.

"A whitetail range element" is any trail, site or area often or regularly used or visited by one or more whitetails. It may be often or regularly used or visited during one or more short periods annually, a grove that produces much-relished white oak acorns, for example, or it may be often or regularly used or visited throughout the period whitetails inhabit individual home ranges (spring through early winter), the bedding area of an adult buck, for example. The cover and/or terrain of a whitetail range element may or may not differ in appearance from the cover and/or terrain of the surrounding area. The location, size and shape of a range element is made evident by certain deer signs, unique and/or obviously more abundant than in the surrounding area. Buck range elements are buck-frequented deer trails (including scrape routes), bedding areas, feeding areas and watering spots.

Johnny-on-the-spot buck hunting derives its effectiveness from hunting at two different sites daily near or within range elements currently frequented by intended quarries, as evidenced by very fresh, identifying deer signs. To key on very fresh, identifying deer signs at two different sites daily, the hunter must scout daily. To insure quarries will pass near selected stand sites during subsequent half-days of hunting, they cannot be alerted or alarmed while the hunter is scouting. To minimize the likelihood of alerting or alarming a quarry, whether scouting during a hunting season or hunting, the hunter must always be aware of where a quarry is most likely to be located at the present time. Such an awareness begins with a knowledge of buck habits and buck range element scouting.

Here again, the word "likely" is involved. No adult buck is predictable enough to allow the hunter to be 100% positive it will be at a certain location at any one time. The most knowledgeable hunter will be wrong at least 10–25% of the time. While mid-hunt scouting, the hunter must constantly run the risk of blundering unexpectedly into an intended quarry at short range. Under such circumstances, adult bucks almost always escape unscathed and then completely disappear until the hunting season is over. Nonetheless, the Johnny-on-the-spot buck hunter must scout daily. Without mid-hunt scouting, this hunting method becomes little more than random, long-stop still-hunting with 1-in-30 odds for success. For me, 1-in-30 odds are unacceptable. I'd much rather work hard at limiting as much as possible the likelihood of alerting or alarming a quarry and always be prepared for the worst by keeping an ace or two in the hole—an extra adult buck or two to hunt should I fail.

At this point the terms "alerting" and "alarming" need to be defined. To understand their meanings, and how they differ, consider the following scenarios—two classic and one characteristic of Johnny-on-the-spot buck hunting:

Scenario 1: via sight, sound and/or airborne scent, a hunter is identified by an adult buck at a range of slightly over 100 yards. Upon assessing the hunter's behavior, it became apparent the hunter was unaware of the buck's presence (the hunter is not acting in a threatening manner). Though potentially dangerous, because the hunter was non-threatening and a safe distance away, the buck was not alarmed, not inclined to flee. Instead it will merely became "alert"—"extra-alert," actually. Shortly, the buck resumed what it was doing, feeding in a leisurely fashion, never moving nearer to the hunter, however, and generally keeping deer-tall cover between itself and the hunter. Finally, the buck walked without haste, stealthily, however, heading toward a favorite watering spot. Though not outwardly apparent, the buck remained "extra-alert" all the while it was within 200 yards of the hunter. Its eyes, ears and nose constantly monitored the hunter's activities, movements and behavior, ever alert to any change that might suggest the hunter has discovered the buck, selected it as a prey and is now stalking nearer. None of this materializing, the buck felt no need to abandon its range or become nocturnal, but over the next ten days, it did not approach within 100 yards of the site where the hunter was discovered and during the following weeks, it never approached within 100 yards without first making certain the hunter was not again at the same site, generally using its nose to assess odors from a safe distance downwind.

Scenario 2: an adult buck unexpectedly discovers a human hunter moving on foot within 100 yards. It appears the hunter will approach to within 50 yards and the hunter is exhibiting threatening or dangerous behavior—moving furtively, stopping often to peer about and listen. The buck is instantly "alarmed," It whirls and moves rapidly away, its first goal, to gain a safe distance of 100 yards or more. Being an adult buck, it attempts to flee without attracting the attention of the hunter. Though the white hairs of its tail and rump are erect, it keeps its tail down and trots, noisily bounding only a last resort. Thoroughly aroused and expecting pursuit, it does not halt its flight until a great distance away, generally off-range, in an area where it has successfully eluded dangerous predators or humans in the past. It remains in this place of proven security over the next ten days, avoiding further threat by remaining bedded in dense cover by day and moving about only at night.

Scenario 3: an adult buck has unexpectedly discovered a seated human (sitting on a stool) 50 yards away. The human did not turn its attention toward the buck (did not gaze toward the deer), made no sounds or discernable moves, exhibiting no threatening behavior. Seemingly resting or sleeping, the potentially dangerous human appeared to have no interest at all in whitetails. Though inclined to flee, this apparent "harmlessness" of the human made rapid flight seem unnecessary, at least for the moment. As moments passed, the human's aura of "harmlessness" unchanging, the frozen buck became more and more confident it had nothing to fear. Soon, it turned and began moving away, *slowly*, halting often to stare back at the hunter. Once a safe distance away, the buck proceeded as if merely "alerted."

Following scenario 1 or 3, the hunter has no chance to take the "alerted" adult buck within 100 yards of the site where identification took place. The odds for taking this buck at sites 100 yards or more away, however, are not materially diminished.

The problem is, though a merely "alerted" adult buck is unlikely to abandon its range and/or become nocturnal, the hunter will not often realize when an adult buck has become merely "alerted." A half-day of fruitless hunting or fresh, disclosing tracks discovered as you leave your stand site may make it obvious your quarry was merely "alerted," obvious why you did not see it, but not until that half-day of hunting is over, wasted. If this scenario is repeated, half-day after half-day, the sunset on the final day of hunting will not appear particularly beautiful.

Scenario 2, of course, is generally a total disaster, the hunter having almost no chance at all of taking that buck throughout the balance of the hunting season.

Thus it is of utmost importance to avoid "alerting" or "alarming" adult bucks..

There are two ways to avoid alerting or alarming an intended quarry while scouting during a hunting season: 1) use adequate stealth and/or 2) scout a likely area while your quarry is somewhere else—scout a feeding area while the buck is bedded, for example. When all else fails, a convincing act of appearing harmless often works, turning a potentially disastrous "alarming" encounter into a mere "alerting" encounter.

Avoiding ruinous alerting or alarming begins with pre-season scouting, or to be more precise, with range element scouting. To locate and identify buck range elements, areas where fresh signs of intended quarries are most likely to be found while hunting, the hunter must first understand whitetail home ranges.

Whitetails do not frequent all suitable habitat in any one region. From early spring until whitetails migrate to wintering areas in December, they limit their activities and movements to specific areas called home ranges.

Adult does and their young, including yearlings (unless the yearling does have young), live in home ranges 80–250 acres in size, averaging about 125 acres. Each adult doe will vigorously defend its home range from being used by other does with young. Within their home ranges, adult does and their young create dense networks of trails (an identifying characteristic), one generally found within fifty yards whatever direction you might walk. Doe ranges are generally well separated. Areas in between, called buffer zones, are little traveled by whitetails, and thus they have few deer trails (an identifying characteristic). Typically, there are four doe home ranges within about a square-mile of suitable habitat.

Adult bucks establish much larger home ranges. In spring, two-year-old bucks typically claim home ranges about 1/2-square-mile in size. Bucks 3–6 years of age claim home ranges 3/4 – 1-1/2 square-miles in size, sometimes larger. Older dominant bucks claim the largest home ranges. Dominant buck home ranges become breeding ranges, vigorously defended from invasion by other antlered bucks, from 2–3 weeks before breeding begins until the 1–2 week primary breeding phase of the rut ends. Unlike doe ranges, buck ranges are not well separated. They tend to overlap other buck ranges. Two or more bucks may share large portions of home ranges. Due to overlapping, as many as 3–5 adult bucks may live within one square-mile. Buck ranges also overlap doe ranges, typically encompassing 2–6 of them and portions of others. When convenient, adult bucks make use of the more-worn trails of doe home ranges, but being aloof and wary loners, they much prefer using their own, less-obvious trails.

Adult bucks do not ordinarily travel throughout their larger home ranges daily. They tend to limit their daily movements to mere fractions of their ranges—a limited number of available home range elements—which for various reasons, natural and hunting-related, change in size and location from time to time. To accurately predict where fresh signs of adult bucks will be found on any one day of hunting, and then find them without alerting or alarming a quarry, the hunter must understand why, where and when such changes take place.

Admittedly, it might seem like we're getting way out in left field somewhere. While gnawing through your share of a jar of pickled pig's feet in deer camp this fall, imagine the response you get, asking, "What do you guys know about changes in range utilization by adult bucks?" After things have quieted down and everyone has wiped away the tears, then ask, "What do you guys know about adult bucks?" You'll probably be able to hear a pin drop. The point is, most hunters know very little about adult bucks, much less range utilization. Though some will pound on tables, insisting they're right, most only guess about anything concerning adult bucks. Rightfully so. Few hunters see enough of adult bucks to learn anything of real hunting value. If you were to ask a hundred deer hunters how to take a big buck, though most have never taken a big buck, practically all of them would tell you to do the same ridiculous thing: "Sit in a tree stand next to a well-used deer trail and use a buck lure." Rest assured, we're not way out in left field. What we're talking about, changes in range utilization by adult bucks, is a highfalutin term for something few deer hunters have but every deer hunter wants. It's called "buck savvy." In that light, I will now do my best to guide you through this enormously important subject.

So here we are: the hunting season begins in three weeks and we are about to begin our fall range element scouting, searching for bedding areas, feeding areas, watering spots and trails that will be frequented by two or three adult bucks during the hunting season. How should we go about it and what should we look for?

If you scouted for suitable quarries earlier (quarry scouting), you know exactly where to begin. If you didn't, begin with a brisk hike, generally following deer trails through every 20–acre area in your hunting area. Moving fast, ignore everything but relatively fresh tracks and droppings. When you find some, measure them (don't guess). When you find some that measure up to "big buck" (see Whitetail Hunter's Almanac, 4th Edition, A Guide to More Than 200 Signs of White-tailed Deer"), take note of where you found them (marking their locations on a self-made or topographical map of your hunting area is a good idea) and then head for another area a half-mile or so away, one well separated from the area you are in, a swamp, clearing, field, road, watercourse, pond, steep elevation or deep depression in between. This will insure any adult-buck-sized tracks or droppings you find in that other area will be those of another adult buck. Differences in measurements will also tell you when you are looking at tracks and droppings of different bucks (the main reason all tracks and droppings should be measured). Once you've located 2–3 suitable quarries, it's time to begin the next step.

Identifying Adult Buck Range Elements

Johnny-on-the-spot buck hunting is a hunting method that minimizes the likelihood of alerting or alarming a quarry, thus minimizing the likelihood of range abandonment. While within its range, each time an adult buck identifies a human hunter at any one location, it will thereafter detour around the surrounding area, roughly circular in shape and 6.5–26 acres in size. Forced to abandon trails or portions of trails that pass through this area and, perhaps, a portion of or all of an adjacent feeding area, the buck will then begin using different trails and, perhaps, a different feeding area. To keep abreast of such changes, you must cautiously scout unhunted portions of the buck's range daily.

To minimize the risk of alerting or alarming your quarry as you scout unhunted areas, you must be able to predict the following: 1) your quarry's likeliest current location, 2) when it will likely leave and 3) its likeliest next destination. To be correct most of the time, to save time and minimize the distances that must be traveled while scouting, you must know considerably more than "whitetails feed early and late in the day and bed midday." A number of factors can greatly alter the hours whitetails are active, weather and phases of the rut the most common.

To make it easy to understand all you should know to accurately predict where whitetails will be, and when, on any one day of a hunting season, something quick and easy to refer to while preparing to scout or hunt, I have created the following chart. It will enable you to accurately predict current locations and next destinations of adult bucks at least 75–90% of the time. This does not necessarily mean you will blunder into selected quarries, alerting or alarming them, 10–25% of the time. When you're wrong, the buck might actually be somewhere else, Whatever the case, proper scouting techniques will minimize the likelihood of ruinous encounters.

To make the following chart fit the small pages of this book, I found it necessary to abbreviate terms. This made it necessary to create a key to abbreviations, which, alas, turns out to be rather lengthy. This may make this chart somewhat cumbersome to use at first, and I apologize for that, but I am sure, in time, you will come to regard this chart as "extremely valuable."

Calendar dates included are derived from my whitetail studies in northern Minnesota. Generally, these dates are applicable to whitetails of southern Canada and the northern tier of U.S. states. South of this region, all rut phases begin later (earlier in Texas). Later dates are attributable to genetic differences between subspecies of whitetails (different biological clocks), differences in climate and differences in the timing of the ratios of darkness to sunlight that trigger all rut phases except phase II. South of the northern tier of U.S. states dates listed should only be considered examples of time spans involved. As explained in earlier books, hunters south of this region should make every effort to replace the dates of this list with dates applicable to personal hunting areas.

Likeliest Current Locations and Next Destinations of Adult Bucks

Key to Abbreviations

RP: rut phase (chart column heading)
CW: current weather (chart column heading)
BC: buck class
TD: time of day (chart column heading)
PL: present location (chart coumn heading)
ND: next destination (chart column heading)

I: rut phase I, the development phase (Sept. 1 – Oct. 15). Beginning with velvet shedding, antlered bucks of each 1–2 square-mile area begin regularly meeting in a certain large feeding area where they engage in sparring and battling late in feeding cycles, each seeking to establish the highest possible position in the local buck hierarchy, the most dominant gaining the opportunity to breed later.

II: rut phase II, the breeding range establishment phase (Oct. 15 – Nov. 3–5). Following 2–3 nights of frosty temperatures, generally 2–3 weeks before does begin experiencing estrus, all antler bucks begin marking breeding ranges, encompassing 1–6 home ranges of adult does, with antler rubs and ground scrapes—easily-spotted, musk-laden markers intended to ward off competitors. Within 3–7 days, the most dominant buck of the area will run off all lesser antlered bucks within its claimed breeding range, forcing them to live temporarily in seclusion in small (typically 20–30 acres) areas, usually off-range. Generally, displaced lesser bucks are loners. Two or more sometimes share temporary ranges (especially the case in crowded farm areas). While the dominant buck patrols its breeding range, ever alert to the presence of any lesser buck that dares sneak back to its former home range, it will renew the musk odors of each of 30–70 ground scrapes, and many antler rubs, along up to 4-1/2 miles of major deer trails coursing through 4–6 (sometimes as many as eight) home ranges of adult does, at least once every

For bucks, breeding-related activities begin with the shedding of velvet.

24–48 hours (unless it is unseasonably warm or it is necessary to detour scrapes frequented by large predators or human hunters). Displaced lesser bucks quickly make and begin regularly renewing the musk odors of ground scrapes and antler rubs along the typically few established deer trails found within their temporary ranges.

Buck depositing urine and tarsal musk on ground scrape.

III: rut phase III, the primary breeding phase (Nov. 3–5 – Nov. 17). Beginning November 3rd, 4th or 5th, sometimes as late as the 7th, about 85% of adult and yearling does are bred during this two-week period (sometimes shorter). Not all does experience estrus at once. Each is in estrus 24–26 hours, about 11% on any one day. From day-one, dominant bucks spend most of their time accompanying does in estrus. While in estrus, does observe normal feeding hours, feeding in their own principle feeding areas within their own home ranges, dominant bucks and young following closely behind. Most breeding occurs midday in doe bedding areas. Meanwhile, because repellant musk odors of dominant buck ground scrapes and antler rubs are waning, some thus-emboldened lesser adult bucks return to former home ranges. In turn, they are drawn by airborne pheromone to does in estrus. Dominant bucks demonstrate their resultant rage by pawing the ground and thrashing saplings, then charging lesser bucks that fail to maintain a desirable distance. Realizing they are in serious peril, most lesser bucks settle for meekly shadowing the breeding pair until the doe no longer exudes the irresistible odor of pheromone.

Buck with doe in estrus

IV: rut phase IV, the recovery phase (a 2–4 week period beginning November 18th) Within 24–48 hours after does no longer emit pheromone, exhausted dominant bucks head back to their bedding areas for much needed seclusion and rest. Lesser antlered bucks (including yearlings) encountered along the way are treated with unaccustomed friendliness. One or more will commonly accompany a dominant buck days at a time, possibly enlisted as sentinels by the weary breeding buck. Adult bucks yet off-range begin returning to former home ranges, all whitetails soon resuming normal habits within normal home ranges. During the first week or two after returning to its bedding area, the dominant buck will not travel a great deal, generally feeding docilely in the path of the nearest adult doe and young, not uncommonly following in their footsteps an hour or so after they have passed. Once rested, though the dominant buck will no longer attempt to maintain an exclusive breeding range, it will occasionally make quick circuits of its scrape trails, renewing few, if any scrapes. This is probably done to find does that breed late.

Buck returned to normal bedding area following primary breeding phase of rut.

V: rut phase V, the supplemental breeding phase (a period lasting up to 42 days, beginning 28 days after the onset of the primary breeding phase) Does not bred during the primary breeding phase of the rut experience estrus again 28 days later (about 10% of does), and 28 days after that if still not bred (about 5% of does). Precocious fawn does experience estrus for the first time 28 days after the onset of the primary breeding phase. Between periods of estrus, adult buck habits and behavior are the same as they are following the first week of rut phase IV. During the 24–26 hours late-breeding does are in estrus, dominant bucks revert to rut phase III behavior, continuing to breed until antlers are shed (generally occurring in late December soon after migrating to wintering areas).

Db: dominant buck, generally the heaviest and most aggressive adult buck in any 0.5–1.5 square-mile area, also usually having the largest antlers; a breeding buck.

Lb: lesser adult buck; a buck 2-1/2 to 6-1/2 years of age that is not the most dominant within the area in which it lives, likely because it is not the heaviest, it doesn't have the largest antlers and/or it is not the most aggressive; generally a non-breeding buck.

MW: moderate or mild weather; temperature normal for the season, winds calm to 14 mph, no precipitation.

SW: stormy weather; winds exceeding 14 mph, steady or gusting, and/or moderate-to-heavy precipitation; any amount of sleet.

WW: wet weather; winds calm to 6 mph and light precipitation—fog, mist, drizzle, light rain or light snow.

UW: unseasonably warm weather.

EM: early morning; first light until 9 or 10 AM.

MM; mid-morning; 9 to 10 AM.

LM: late morning; 11 am to noon.

EA: early afternoon; 3–4 hours before sunset.

LA: late afternoon; 1–2 hours before sunset.

SS: sunset.

AD: anytime of day.

Dbba: dominant buck bedding area.

Lbba: lesser buck bedding area.

Tlbba: temporary lesser buck bedding area; a bedding area, not necessarily well defined, of a lesser adult buck while living within its small temporary range during phases II and III of the rut.

Bfa: buck feeding area; may or may not be shared by antlerless deer

Psfa: post-storm feeding area, typically near a bedding area; when strong winds (steady or gusting) and/or moderate-to-heavy precipitation forces deer to remain bedded during normal feeding hours, deer begin feeding (adult bucks take to scrape routes during rut phase II) within minutes after wind becomes calm or light and precipitation becomes light or ends, whatever the time of day except when occurring within 1–2 hours the next feeding cycle.

Tlbfa: temporary lesser buck feeding area; a feeding area, not necessarily well defined, of a lesser adult buck while living within its small temporary range during phases II and III of the rut.

Bws: buck watering spot.

Dba: doe bedding area.

Dfa: doe feeding area; feeding area of doe and young, including fawns, yearling does without young and yearling bucks.

Dws: doe watering spot.

Dbsr: dominant buck scrape route; a series of regularly-freshened ground scrapes found along major deer trails *within* boundaries of doe home ranges.

Lbsr: scrape route of lesser adult buck; a series of regularly-freshened ground scrapes found along a deer trail *outside* of boundaries of doe home ranges; generally found within the small temporary range of a lesser buck after its has been driven from its home range by a dominant buck at the onset of rut phase II.

NA: not applicable; will arrive at next destination after legal shooting hours.

RP	CW	BC	TD	PL	ND
I	MW	DB/LB	EM–MM	Bfa	Bws
		DB	MM	Bws	Dbba
		LB	MM	Bws	Lbba
		DB	MM–LA	Dbba	Bfa
		LB	MM–LA	Lbba	Bfa
		DB/LB	LA–SS	Bfa	NA
	SW	DB	AD	Dbba	Psfa
		LB	AD	Lbba	Psfa
	WW	DB/LB	EM–LM	Bfa	Bws
		DB	LM	Bws	Dbba
		LB	LM	Bws	Lbba
		DB	LM–EA	Dbba	Bfa
		LB	LM–EA	Lbba	Bfa
		DB/LB	EA–SS	Bfa	NA
II	MW	DB	EM–MM	Dbsr	Dbba
		LB	EM–MM	Lbsr	Tlbba
		DB	MM–LA	Dbba	Dbsr
		LB	MM–LA	Tlbba	Lbsr
		DB	LA–SS	Dbsr	NA
		LB	LA–SS	Lbsr	NA
	SW	DB	AD	Dbba	Dbsr
		LB	AD	Tlbba	Lbsr
	WW	DB	EM–SS	Dbsr	NA
		LB	EM–SS	Lbsr	NA
	UW	DB	EM-SS	Dbba	NA
		LB	EM–SS	Tlbba	NA
III	MW	DB	EM–MM	Dfa	Dws
		DB	MM	Dws	Dba
		LB	EM–MM	Tlbba*	Tlbba*
		DB	MM–LA	Dba	Dfa
		LB	MM–LA	Tlbba*	Tlbba*
		DB	LA–SS	Dfa	NA

		LB	LA–SS	Tlbfa	NA
	SW	DB	AD	Dba	Dfa
		LB	AD	Tlbba*	Tlbfa*
	WW	DB	EM–LM	Dfa	Dba
		LB	EM–LM	Tlbfa*	Tlbba*
		DB	LM–EA	Dba	Dfa
		LB	LM–EA	Tlbba*	Tlbfa*
		DB	EA–SS	Dfa	NA
		LB	EA–SS	Tlbfa*	NA
IV	MW	DB/LB	EM–MM	Bfa**	Bws**
		DB	MM	Bws	Dbba
		LB	MM	Bws**	Lbba**
		DB	MM–LA	Dbba	Bfa
		LB	MM–LA	Lbba**	Bfa**
		DB/LB	LA–SS	Bfa**	NA
	SW	DB	AD	Dbba	Bfa
		LB	AD	Lbba**	Bfa**
	WW	DB	EM–LM	Bfa±	Bws
		LB	EM–LM	Bfa**	Bws**
		DB	LM	Bws	Dbba
		LB	LM	Bws**	Lbba**
		DB	LM–EA	Dbba	Bfa
		LB	LM–EA	Lbba**	Bfa**
		DB/LB	EA–SS	Bfa**	NA
V	MW	DB/LB	EM–MM	Bfa	Bws
				or	
				Dfa‡	Dws‡
		DB	MM	Bws	Dbba
				or	
				Dws‡	Dba‡
		LB	MM	Bws	Lbba
				or	
				Dws‡	Dba‡
		DB	MM–LA	Dbba	Bfa
				or	
				DBA‡	DFA‡
		LB	MM–LA	LBBA	BFA
				or	
				Dba‡	Dfa‡
		DB/LB	LA–SS	Bfa	NA
				or	
				Dfa‡	NA

SW	DB	AD	Dbba		Bfa
				or	
			Dba‡		Dfa‡
	LB	AD	Lbba		Bfa
				or	
			Dba‡		Dfa‡
WW	DB/LB	EM–LM	Bfa		Bws
				or	
			Dfa‡		Dws‡
	DB	LM	Bws		Dbba
				or	
			Dws‡		Dba‡
	LB	LM	Bws		Lbba
				or	
			Dws‡		Dba‡
	DB	LM–EA	Dbba		Bfa
				or	
			Dba‡		Dfa‡
	LB	LM–EA	Lbba		Bfa
				or	
			Dba‡		Dfa‡
	DB/LB	EA–SS	Bfa		NA
				or	
			Dfa‡		NA

* Lesser buck may trail dominant buck with doe in estrus.
** Lesser buck may accompany dominant buck.
± Dominant buck may make quick circuit of previously established scrape routes.
‡ If accompanying a late-breeding doe in estrus.

Locating and Identifying Range Elements of Adult Bucks

In the chart above, there are twelve categories of range elements. You task now is to find them in your hunting area.

Range elements of a single adult buck will typically include one bedding area, several watering spots, up to two dozen feeding areas and more than one-hundred trails. If you plan to be prepared to hunt three adult bucks and if it was necessary to identify every range element used by those bucks from early spring to early winter, you'd have to find roughly 400 range elements. Fortunately, most of those range elements can be weeded out. All you really need to find are range elements currently frequented by quarries—trails and sites where fresh deer signs of quarries are most abundant right now—applicable to opening morning hunting and those likely to be frequented by quarries during the balance of the period you plan to hunt them.

It doesn't take a crystal ball to identify range elements likely to be frequented by adult bucks after the first half-day of a hunting season. Some will be the same as those frequented now (2–3 weeks before the opener), bedding areas and waterings spots, for example. Some will be recognized via year-old deer signs and/or by remembering where identifying signs were located during the same period you hunted whitetails in the area a year earlier, scrape routes and browse areas, for example. Others will be recognized via features that fit the needs of adult bucks during hunting seasons.

Though you will doubtless fail to discover and identify some potentially productive buck range elements, you should have no difficulty finding at least one new stand site that will put you within 100 yards of a adult buck during every half-day you plan to hunt and that's only the beginning. Once you begin mid-hunt scouting, you'll find an endless number of stand sites near trails or sites frequented by your quarry right now, including any important stand sites you may miss while scouting before the opener. And wherever they are, since you do not have to prepare a stand site in any way, you'll be completely free to hunt any promising new stand site you discover at any time.

Identifying signs of the range elements you should find are as follows:

Adult Buck Bedding Areas

The are three reasons why it is especially important to know the locations of bedding areas of adult bucks.

First, a bedding area is the hub, the center, the starting place and the ending place for all of an adult buck's activities and movements. Except during rut phase III while breeding is in progress, at no place in its vast range is a dominant buck, one of the biggest bucks in your hunting area, more predictable, both in location and time. Except during rut phases II and III, at no place in its vast range is any other adult buck more predictable, both in location and time.

Second, as long as an adult buck is secure in its bedding area or as long as no hunter exhibits hunting behavior or deposits fresh trail scents within 100 yards or so of an adult buck's bedding area (following pre-season scouting), that buck will not change the location of its bedding area, and though it may alter the timing of its habits and/or limit daylight movements to less and less range area, it will remain within its home or breeding range. Only an unexpected, short-range encounter with a human or a fearsome human thunderbolt (gunshot) at close range will make the buck seek refuge off-range for an extended period of time.

Third, mid-hunt scouting is much more productive and far less risky when the hunter knows the location of a quarry's bedding area. During the hours an adult buck is normally bedded, as long as a quarry's bedding area is avoided, approached no nearer than 200 yards, the hunter can scout almost anywhere, exercising only a minimum of caution (stealth) without fear of alerting or alarming the quarry.

If you are starting out cold, unaware of locations of bedding areas of the adult bucks you plan to hunt, you can save yourself a lot of leg work by studying a topographical map of your hunting area first. Bedding areas of adult bucks have characteristics that will usually fit certain areas on such a map, narrowing the search.

Each spring, adult bucks select bedding areas that will give them the best chance of avoiding rapid flight during the coming four months—the antler growing season. Rapid flight is especially hazardous to the rubbery beams and the soft, blood-rich covering (velvet) of developing antlers—a buck's most coveted possession. To eliminate or minimize the need for rapid flight, an adult buck's bedding area must provide effective concealment, a means of detecting the approach of large predators or man at distances great enough to allow a leisurely escape and a ready means of discouraging pursuit.

Secluded bedding area provides protection for developing antlers.

Clever concealment is the hallmark of an adult white-tailed buck, and when it comes to concealing bedding areas, they're at their very best. To make their bedding areas difficult to find, unlikely to be stumbled upon, they keep them small, generally an acre or two in size (sometimes as large as 10 acres in size). Hidden deep in dense cover, adult buck bedding areas are located well away from paths frequented by other deer, large predators and man.

To further reduce the likelihood of discovery during the antler growing season, adult bucks feed and water within or very near their bedding areas, minimizing exposure and limiting the spread of revealing trail scents.

A reliable source of water—a spring or spring-fed basin, stream, river, pond, lake or swamp—is generally located within 200 yards.

Effective concealment, of course, is a two-way street. If an approaching predator or man can't see a bedded buck, the bedded buck can't see the approaching predator or man. Adult bucks go to extraordinary lengths to make sure predators or man cannot stalk near without being scented or heard at safe distances, especially heard, hearing never handicapped by dense cover or an unfavorable wind direction. Where high hills, bluffs or mountains are present, adult bucks generally bed on or near the tops on wooded benches or saddles (in areas not accessible via motor vehicle) where they have a grand view of at least half of the surrounding area. In other regions adult bucks generally bed low, within or adjacent to lowlands where wet or damp soil supports dense growths of woody shrubs and trees. Whether high or low, bedding areas of adult bucks are characteristically buried within sizable patches of very dense, woody cover, cover characteristically impossible for a large predator or man to penetrate without making sounds that can be heard a good distance away. Older bucks are particularly fond of bedding among windfalls—long-dead, fallen trees bristling with brittle branches that snap, crackle or pop when disturbed. Such an alarm system is usually so effective that adult bucks rarely find it necessary to flee from their beds in haste. Nonetheless, adult bucks are always prepared for the worst, characteristically bedding adjacent to cover or terrain that quickly discourages pursuit by large predators or man—large, wooded swamps, steep and treacherous slopes or posted land, for example.

Buck bedding areas are generally located within 200 yards of water.

Bedding areas of adult bucks must also provide comfort, dry spots for bedding and mature trees for protection from wind, rain and midsummer's blazing sun. Among these trees are generally at least a few evergreens or shrubs that will provide a protective canopy after most deciduous trees have lost their leaves in autumn.

With these characteristics in mind, you can now look at your topographical map and begin picking out areas where you are most likely to find bedding areas of adult bucks. Though not all sources of water will be delineated on your map, you can start by eliminating all areas not within 200 yards of water. You can also eliminate all areas not colored green— non-wooded areas. Also swamps. Don't eliminate small islands and ridges surrounded by swamps, however, especially those located within 100-200 yards of large highlands (very common buck bedding areas). If you hunt in high hills, bluffs or mountains, be sure to put an "X" on each wooded saddle or bench (a flat area sticking out on one side) on or near crests in areas inaccessible by motor vehicle; also headwaters of streams in high valleys.

Begin scouting by keying on X's within 800 yards (about 1/2 mile) of the sites where you initially discovered fresh adult-buck-sized tracks and/ or droppings. This map approach may not lead you to every buck bedding area, but as you'll happily discover, it will lead you quickly to many. If you don't find a buck bedding area where expected, all you can do is cruise through every likely area within 800 yards of the site where you found the buck's tracks of droppings, keeping your eyes peeled for topography, cover and deer signs characteristic of bedding areas of adult bucks. Keep in mind, bedding areas of adult bucks may or may not be located within home ranges of adult does. They may be buried in areas only traveled by buck's, trails lightly used and choked with trailside cover.

Several deer signs characterize buck bedding areas. The first and most obvious sign you're likely to spot is an antler rub. The appearance of the rub, its relative age and the diameter of the tree it's on depends on when you scout.

If you scout before September 1st, all rubs will be old, a year or more in age.

If you scout between September 1st and 2 or 3 weeks before breeding begins, the only fresh rubs you're likely to find are velvet rubs. Most bucks rub off velvet on 1–3 saplings or woody shrubs with trunks an inch or less in diameter. A velvet rub may be found on a single sapling that has suffered no more damage than having a two-foot section of bark stripped off or it might be a clump of saplings or brush that appears to have been savagely beaten with the edge of a shovel, bark shredded, branches broken and dangling. Velvet rubs do not reflect sizes of bucks, but they are generally found very near or within a buck bedding area.

If you scout later, you'll spot fresh rubs on large-diameter trees almost everywhere you go. These rubs do reflect the size of the buck. At this time, adult bucks 2-1/2 years of age generally rub on tree trunks 1-1/2 – 2-1/2 inches in diameter and 3-1/3 – 6-1/2 year-old bucks rub on tree trunks 3–6 inches in diameter, sometimes larger. Most large-diameter antler rubs are made during the 2–3 week period before breeding begins. They are scent laden breeding range markers intended to ward off other antlered bucks. Within a few days after this phase of the rut begins, dominant bucks will run off all lesser bucks, whereupon lesser bucks will begin making rubs within *their* 20–30 acre temporary quarters off-range. Restless and com-

A dominant buck in its bedding area, surrounded by antler rubs.

bative during this rut phase, rather than lie down in their bedding areas during usual bedding hours, dominant bucks, especially, stage mock battles with trees. They'll make 6–30 thirty large-diameter rubs in their bedding areas during this calendar period. Wherever you find an antler rub, therefore, fresh or old, slender velvet rub or large-diameter rub, search the immediate vicinity for more. If you find six or more rubs clustered in a 1–2 acre area,.you are likely standing in the bedding area of an adult buck. To be sure, search for other characteristic signs.

Adult-buck-sized beds are definitive signs of buck bedding areas. Until snow covers the ground, however, they can be difficult to find and measure. Beneath the characteristically-dense, woody cover of a buck bedding area, ground cover is generally too sparse to make easily-distinguished beds. Unless wet, even a layer of fallen leaves will not hold the impression of a bed very long, the leaves generally springing up and erasing a bed within 30 minutes after it is abandoned. When beds are visible, outlines sharp, I always measure them. In the region I hunt, 2-1/2 year-old bucks have beds measuring 45 inches in length, plus or minus an inch or two, and 3-1/2 – 6-1/2 year-old bucks have beds measuring 50–56 inches. I have not found many 56-inch beds, but bucks taken that made such beds always weighed 325-350 pounds, live. That's BIG.

Few trails, rarely major deer trails, cross bedding areas of adult bucks. Most deer movements within a buck bedding area are off-trail. A distinguishing characteristic, then, is a lot of off-trail tracks (you must search off-trail to find them). Tracks, fresh and old, will be everywhere, most if not all of them, one large size.

The first thing a buck does upon rising from a bed is empty its bowels. Another characteristic sign of a buck bedding area, then, is lots of off-trail droppings, fresh and old, most if not all, one large size.

If it's all there—proper topography, dense woody cover, a nearby escape area, nearby water, a cluster of large-diameter antler rubs, large beds, lots of off-trail tracks, fresh and old, and lots of off-trail droppings, fresh and old—it's the bedding area of an adult buck and should hereafter be treated as such.

Dominant Buck Bedding Areas

Characteristic signs of a dominant buck bedding area include lots of the largest off-trail tracks...

Though unlikely to become apparent until buck-class signs have been measured elsewhere, the bedding area of a dominant buck will be characterized by the largest tracks, droppings and beds in the area, and the greatest number of the largest-diameter antler rubs, most on trees three inches or more in diameter (there may be a few on smaller-diameter trees). Upon discovering such a bedding area you will typically say to yourself, "I never knew this place existed," being a ridge buried 100 yards back in a wooded swamp, for example, or "Who would have

lots of the largest off-trail droppings...   *and the largest beds in the area.*

ever thought a buck would bed here?" a brushy rimrock or saddle just below or on the crest of a baldtop mountain, for example. After looking the area over you are also likely to say, "I can understand why a buck would bed here. It would be impossible to sneak near without the buck knowing it." I have uttered these very words many times.

Lesser Adult Buck Bedding Areas

Though obviously the bedding area of an adult buck, the bedding area of a "lesser" adult buck can be difficult to distinguish from the bedding area of a dominant buck until signs of other buck bedding areas have been found and measured. Generally, tracks, droppings and beds will be somewhat smaller. Because lesser adult bucks are usually run off early during the period when more than 90% of antler rubs are made (rut phase II), there will be fewer antler rubs, typically six or less, not including 1–3 one-inch-diameter velvet rubs. A cluster of freshy made rubs on tree trunks 1-1/2 – 2-1/2 inches in diameter identify the bedding area of a 2-1/2 year-old buck.

Lesser Adult Buck Bedding Areas During Rut Phases II and III

Upon being ejected from breeding ranges of dominant bucks during the first days of rut phase II, lesser adult bucks settle in secluded 20–30 acre ranges. Such ranges are either a short distance off-range or within non-doe-range corners of previously established home ranges that are not claimed as breeding range territory by dominant bucks. Typically, displaced lesser bucks quickly make new antler rubs and ground scrapes short distances apart along the few deer trails found in such ranges. They decorate their bedding areas with antler rubs as well, but because there are usually so many rubs scattered about the area, it can be difficult to distinguish their bedding areas via rubs alone. Adult-buck-sized beds and concentrated tracks and droppings off-trail are about the only reliable signs. Adding to the difficulty, rather than bed regularly at one site, lesser adult bucks commonly bed at a number of sites scattered throughout their temporary ranges. When hunting such an area, therefore, the buck's entire 20-30 acre range should be treated as if it is a buck bedding area.

Adult Buck Feeding Areas

The Johnny-on-the-spot buck hunter is a highly skilled ambusher, success dependent on the ability to be in paths of unsuspecting adult bucks at right times. Such a hunter will occasionally discover opportunities to take adult bucks midday while whitetails are normally bedded, but most deer will be ambushed early (best) or late in the day, while whitetails are moving toward feeding areas, about feeding areas or away from feeding areas regardless of which of the five breeding-related activities adult bucks may be engaged in. To be in paths of adult bucks, at the outset of each half-day of hunting, the Johnny-on-the-spot buck hunter must know a quarry's likeliest current location and its likeliest next destination. Invariably, one will be a feeding area. Before begin-ning each half-day of hunting, then, the hunter must know where a quarry is currently feeding.

To illustrate the importance of knowing where whitetails are currently feeding, consider the following example of a classic error made by more than a quarter-million Minnesota firearm deer hunters every fall.

When the hunting season began last fall, the first Saturday in November, Minnesota firearm hunters again discovered whitetails had made some dramatic changes during the 2-3 week interim between pre-season scouting and the opener. Earlier, bucks were in a frenzy of making antler rubs and ground scrapes and all deer were gorging on grasses, clover and such in more open areas where such plants are most abundant. Accordingly, Minnesota forests rang with the sounds of pounding and sawing by excited hunters preparing tree stands overlooking ground scrapes and the more open areas where deer were feeding.

Two or three weeks later, more than two of every three hunters headed home with nothing more than the usual excuses—*the wind was wrong, there wasn't enough snow, there weren't enough hunters, the wolves ate all the bucks, the DNR lied about how many deer there are, etc., etc.* The real reasons so many hunters were not successful were the same two reasons they were not successful the year before and the year before that: 1) does were in estrus opening weekend and bucks were therefore no longer maintaining ground scrapes and 2) whitetails were now feeding on browse. As always, the primary breeding phase of the rut (rut phase III) began November 3rd, 4th or 5th, and, as always, whitetails switched to browse at the end of the first week in November.

Hunters who knew this would happen and thus keyed on downwind perimeters of previously favored browse areas took deer. Some took adult bucks, having found themselves in browse areas in home ranges of adult does currently in estrus.

The point is, you can't expect to be a regularly successful whitetail hunter if you do not anticipate changes in locations of feeding areas.

Factors that cause adult bucks (and other whitetails) to change feeding areas fall under two categories: 1) "natural," generally triggering long-term changes that begin on roughly the same calendar dates annually (whether hunting is in progress or not), and 2) "hunting," generally triggering short-term changes, bucks changing feeding areas or portions of feeding areas one to three times daily if necessary (feeding only at night if safe feeding areas cannot be found during daylight hours).

Feeding areas used by adult bucks as a result of (or in response to) natural factors tend to have unique, identifiable characteristics. Such feeding areas are generally visited by bucks once or twice daily over a period of 2–6 weeks, generally the same 2–6 weeks annually unless the area is destroyed by fire, logging, road construction, flooding (beaver dams), increasing shade from maturing highland timber (mature timber generally enhances the growth of favored whitetail foods in wet lowlands) or smothered by second-growth timber (especially aspen). To accommodate twice-daily feeding over a 2–6 week period, a feeding area must be relatively large (10–40 acres), seasonally favored foods must be abundant and the area must provide adult-buck-class security.

Greater size and more abundant food contribute to the greater security usually sought by super-wary adult bucks. Unlike does, yearlings and fawns, adult bucks seem bent to avoid creating trails loaded with tracks and scents, as if realizing such trails will attract undue attention from dreaded predators or man. The larger the feeding area and the more abundant the food, the less a buck will find it necessary to feed along paths used before and the sooner a buck can eat its fill, thus bring-

Being large and brushy and having a treacherous slope on one side, this is a favorite feeding area of several adult bucks

ing an end the period of greater vulnerability. While feeding, its head down, its mouth noisily ripping or nipping off and chewing food, an adult buck cannot easily see or hear a predator or human stalking near. For this reason, adult bucks commonly feed downwind, insuring they will smell danger stalking their fresh backtrails. Zigzagging from side to side as it feeds, yet moving steadily in one general direction, a feeding buck will not only make it difficult for a a predator or human to trail near, but difficult for either enemy to set up an ambush.

Unless among other feeding deer (not uncommon during phase I of the rut), during hunting seasons especially, adult bucks also seem bent to avoid full exposure while feeding during daylight hours. They much prefer feeding areas loaded with deer-tall (or taller) screening cover. Even better is a feeding area loaded with deer-tall cover that is located next to an effective escape area—a large area of very dense cover and/or difficult-to-travel terrain that quickly exhausts shorter-legged and less-acrobatic pursuers.

As in a buck bedding area, a buck feeding area will be loaded with adult-buck-sized tracks and droppings, fresh and old, on and off-trail. Likely to be shared by one or more other adult bucks and at least one adult doe with young, abundant smaller tracks and droppings, fresh and old, on and off-trail will also be present.

Bored, more quickly sated fawns commonly lie down and chew their cuds while their mothers feed. A few 30-36 inch-long fawn beds may thus be discovered within a buck feeding area, but rarely the 45–56 inch-long beds of adult bucks (a characteristic that differentiates a buck feeding area from a buck bedding area).

Particularly when shared by adult does with young, adult buck feeding areas are also characterized by great numbers of obvious (well-worn) deer trails (another characteristic that differentiates buck feeding areas from buck bedding areas). Like spokes of a bicycle wheel, approach trails converge from all directions. Back in surrounding cover, a well-worn perimeter trail rings the entire area. Major deer trails blanket the feeding area, connected at short, irregular intervals by less-obvious minor deer trails.

While deer are feeding, most movements will be off of established trails. Where visible (in snow or soft soil), tracks of individual deer will not trace straight lines like those of deer traveling toward distant destinations. Tracks will zigzag, deer turning to new sources of food at random intervals, the deer seemingly in no hurry to go somewhere else.

Beginning 2–3 weeks before breeding begins, adult bucks mark their feeding areas with antler rubs. Though feeding area antler rubs tend not to be as numerous as along major deer trails within home ranges of adult does, both antler rubs and buck ground scrapes are regular features of all feeding areas shared or used exclusively by adult does and young. Rubs are usually widely separated and located adjacent to major deer trails, not clustered off-trail in small, 1–2 acre areas as in buck bedding areas (another differentiating characteristic).

Signs most characteristic of feeding areas, of course, are the nipped-off stems of the plants whitetails have eaten, found from ground level to about six feet above the ground. While whitetails are feeding on plants such as grasses and clover, actual evidence of feeding can be difficult to spot. However, if zigzag trails of individual deer are noted in grass, if off-trail tracks and droppings, fresh and old, are abundant, deer have not only eaten the grass, but they have often returned to the site to eat more grass. This is therefore a favorite, long-term, currently frequented feeding area of one or more specific whitetails.

Leaves and green stems nipped off by whitetails are easily seen.

Spring, summer and fall, whitetails feed almost exclusively on greens—leaves and stems of grasses, clover and other ground cover and young green leaves and non-woody stems of various woody saplings, shrubs and trees. Where deer have been devouring leaves of saplings, shrubs and trees, nipped-off stems will usually be quite evident.

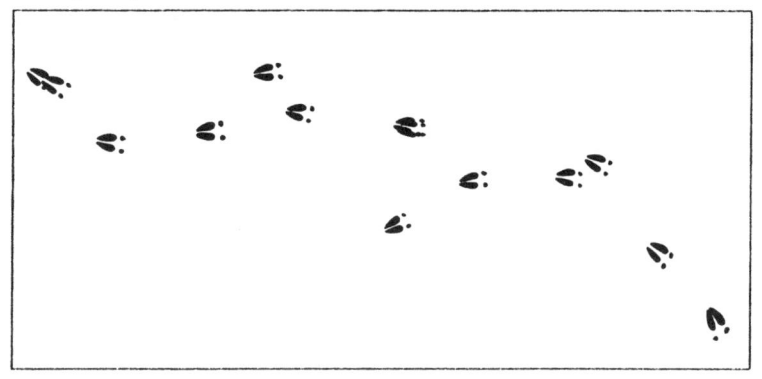

Zigzag tracks typical of a feeding whitetail

When greens are no longer available, whitetails turn to browse—less-fibrous tips and buds of woody saplings, shrubs and trees. Nipped-off stems can hardly be missed, white tips contrasting sharply within surrounding vegetation.

White tips of nipped-off browse plants make it relatively easy to identify and determine the extent of a whitetail feeding (browse) area. Like tiny white flowers, they will blanket favorite, long-term feeding areas. If adult-buck-sized tracks and droppings, fresh and old, on and off-trail, are abundant beneath the white tips, tracks zigzagging, it is currently a favorite or "principle" feeding area of an adult buck.

White tips of nipped off stems of woody shrubs and sapplings identify browse areas.

The preceding explanation of why many Minnesota whitetail hunters fail to take deer each fall points out the fact that it is also important to be able to recognize "previously favored" browse areas well before whitetails begin eating browse. While scouting in August, September or October, browse plants favored by adult bucks will not be characterized by stems with easily-spotted white tips. In fact, previously-favored browse areas may be completely devoid of fresh deer signs of any kind. Nonetheless, if you know what to look for, previously favored browse areas are easily identified.

When a whitetail nips off the stem of a woody browse plant, the entire stem, a portion of the stem or the tip of the stem dies, becoming dark brown or black. The following spring, as leaves begin to emerge, a live, nipped-off stem will generate one or more new stems, originating from buds below the nipped-off tip. If stems of a browse plant are nipped off winter after winter, forcing the plant to regenerate new

Years of feeding give favorite shrubs of winter browse areas this characteristic appearance.

stems spring after spring, the woody plant will become gnarled, knobby and stunted in appearance, perhaps appearing diseased. In early fall, a much-browsed plant will have a mixture of stems, some completely dead and blackened with no leaves, some with blackened tips only with normal leaves below, and some normal and healthy throughout with leaves growing all the way to non-woody green tips (new browse for the coming winter). Any area with great numbers of one-to-six-foot-tall woody plants that fit this description is a future, regularly-visited browse area, *no doubt about it*. If the area is large, the size of a football field or larger, or a very long (50 x 200 yards, for example), if it would be difficult to spot a buck much more than fifty yards away in much of the area (after leaves have fallen), if it borders on or is very near to a large area of cover or terrain you'd just as soon avoid (a wooded swamp or very steep slope, for example) and if it is located within 100 yards of a trail or site where you discovered relatively fresh tracks and/or droppings of an adult buck, that browse area will be frequented by that buck after whitetails begin feeding on browse in early winter, *no doubt about it.*

It is now necessary to introduce and define another new term: "principle feeding area.". A principle feeding area (I prefer the word "principle" over "primary") is one that is regularly visited or frequented by one or more whitetails over a period of two or more weeks. Contingent on the phase of the rut and foods available—greens or browse—feeding areas most likely to be principle for adult bucks are those that have great size, abundant food, abundant screening cover and an adjacent escape area.

Keep in mind, "principle" does not mean "only." It means "most visited" or "most preferred" while safe. "Safe" means winds are calm-to-light, the wind direction is favorable and precipitation is absent or light, making it easy to identify and avoid danger at safe distances. "Safe" means no hunting predators or humans are lurking nearby. Any time a "principle" feeding area is unsafe, adult bucks always have at least one or two "less visited" or "less-preferred" feeding areas to use. If none are safe, adult bucks routinely take quick advantage one or both of two other effective options: 1) though preferred foods my be limited at any one site and widely scattered, they begin feeding almost anywhere else and/or 2) they begin feeding only at night, thus able to feed anywhere they want in complete safety (discounting poachers), including "most preferred" feeding areas. Whether scouting, planning a hunt, or hunting, therefore, never handicap yourself by believing a buck will (or must) feed in only one specific area. Also, never hunt a buck feeding area without doing your utmost to make certain your quarry will continue to consider the area "safe."

Included in the above definition are the words "over a period of two or more weeks." From about September 1st until whitetails begin migrating to wintering areas, adult bucks frequent several principle feeding areas. Normally, each is frequented 2–6 weeks, and as long as foods and cover hold up, the same feeding areas are frequented by adult bucks during the same 2–6 weeks, year after year. There is one notable exception. During the 2–3 week period before breeding begins (rut phase II) and during the two-week primary breeding phase of the rut (rut phase III), dominant bucks have no principle feeding areas.

To make it easier for you to understand, locate and identify principle feeding areas of adult bucks, I have created the following condensed guide. As before, each period (calendar dates) listed is most applicable to hunting in southern Canada, Minnesota and other states bordering Canada. The term "principle basis"—a rut phase—alludes to the main reason a principle feeding area of one or more adult bucks is located where it is during a specific time period. To review activities of adult bucks during rut phases listed, see the key to abbreviations under "Likeliest Current Locations and Next Destinations of Adult Bucks" (page 36).

Principle Feeding Areas of Adult Bucks

Principle Feeding Area No. 1

Period: Sept. 1 – Oct. 15

Principle basis: rut phase I

Principle food: greens— grasses, clover and other leafy, non-woody plants and leaves and stems of various woody saplings, shrubs and trees. Whitetails gorge on greens at this time of year to accumulate the fat stores needed to survive the coming winter.

Location: within one or more ranges (overlapping) of adult bucks (identified by the presence of fresh, adult-buck-class deer signs).

General description: a fairly large area, 10–40 acres in size, where sunlight can regularly bathe much of the ground (such as a clearcut), promoting the abundant growth of green and leafy plants inches to five or six feet tall.

While whitetails are consuming grasses, clover and such, it is difficult to spot physical evidences of feeding.

Identifying deer signs: 1) obviously greater numbers of adult-buck-sized tracks and droppings of various sizes (lengths), fresh and old, on and off-trail (the only other area in which as many off-trail buck tracks will be found is a buck bedding area), 2) zigzag trails (feeding bucks move from side to side, intervals between turns, short and irregular) and 3) signs of sparring or battling bucks—patches (typically oblong, 10–40 feet long) of heavily trampled or scuffed-up soil and turf.

Principle Feeding Area No. 2

Period: Oct. 16 – Nov. 3–5
Principle basis: rut phase II
Principle food: greens—grasses, clover and other non-woody plants protected from killer frosts by fallen leaves, dense overhead cover or standing water (in wet lowlands or bordering swamps, ponds, lakes, streams or rivers).

Patches of soil trampled by battling bucks identify buck feeding areas during September and the first weeks of October.

Location: *dominant bucks* have no principle feeding areas during this period. While patrolling breeding ranges, primarily during the hours whitetails normally feed, they snack along scrape routes and sometimes pause briefly to feed with or near adult does and young in their current principle feeding areas. *Lesser adult bucks* may or may not have well-defined principle feeding areas during this period. After rampaging dominant bucks have forced them to vacate entire or large portions of their homes ranges, they temporarily settle within 20–30 acre areas outside of home ranges of adult does (areas not claimed as breeding ranges by dominant bucks). Like bedding areas during the antler growing season, these ranges must provide adequate food, water and security from large predators and man; also security from brutish dominant bucks and a trail or two along which they can satisfy instincts for establishing and maintaining breeding ranges (making antler rubs and ground scrapes). Such areas are not frequented by adult does and young because they are fronted by habitat hazardous to travel by fawns or because favored foods are too sparse to support long-term feeding by two or more deer (an adult doe with one or more fawns and one or more yearlings). In the latter case, the adult buck will be forced to feed throughout the area, rarely at any site twice in a row. Even where well-defined feeding areas do exist, like dominant bucks, lesser adult bucks are likely to restlessly prowl their limited scrape routes during feeding cycles, grabbing trailside snatches of greens between pauses to apply fresh scalp and tarsal musk to antler rubs and ground scrapes.

General description: *dominant bucks* and most *lesser adult bucks* do not make use of principle buck feeding areas during this period. Main sources of food, scrape routes and principle feeding areas of adult does with young are described later in this chapter. Where principle buck feeding areas exist within temporary ranges of displaced lesser bucks, they are most commonly found in wet lowlands bordering running or standing water.

Identifying deer signs: signs of feeding areas of *dominant bucks* include: 1) fresh adult-buck-sized tracks and droppings, zigzagging tracks, on or near scrape trails (ground scrapes regularly freshened) within home ranges of adult does and on or near buffer zone trails connecting adult doe home ranges and 2) fresh adult-buck-sized tracks and droppings among abundant zigzagging tracks of deer with fawn-to-adult-doe-sized tracks and droppings, fresh and old, on and off-trail (signs of principle feeding areas of adult does and young). Signs of principle feeding areas of *lesser adult bucks* are fresh, adult-buck-sized tracks and droppings of adult bucks, zigzagging tracks, on or near scrape trails in areas not ordinarily frequented by adult does (may be used as escape areas by adult does and young during hunting seasons).

Principle Feeding Area No. 3

Period: Nov. 3–17
Principle basis: rut phase III
Principle food: Nov. 3–7, unless covered by six or more inches of snow, greens—grasses, clover and other non-woody plants protected from killer frosts by fallen leaves, dense overhead cover or standing or running water; Nov. 7–17, browse—woody stems and buds of saplings, shrubs and trees (primarily red osier, black ash saplings, mountain maples and occasionally white cedar and tops of young evergreens in northern Minnesota).

Location: feeding fitfully, if at all,, *dominant bucks* closely trail adult or yearling does in estrus as they feed during usual hours in principle feeding areas of adult does (within home ranges of adult does). *Lesser adult bucks* that have returned to former home ranges also feed fitfully, if at all, shadowing breeding pairs about principle feeding areas of adult does. *Lesser adult bucks* that remain off-range, feed normally during

While breeding is in progress, hunt dominant bucks where they spend most of their time—in feeding and bedding areas of does in estrus.

normal hours near scrape routes or, where they exist, within principle buck feeding areas within their isolated, temporary haunts.

Description: Nov. 3–7, during feeding cycles, ***dominant bucks*** accompanying does in estrus, and ***lesser adult bucks*** that follow them, are found primarily where the few remaining greens exist, in wet, brushy lowlands or edges of swamps, ponds, lakes, streams or rivers in home ranges of adult does; Nov. 8–17, during feeding cycles, these same bucks, are found with does in estrus feeding in large patches or strips of browse, mostly in wet, brushy lowlands or brushy edges of swamps, ponds, lakes, streams or rivers, but also in brushy edges of stands of hardwoods where favored saplings (such as white oak) or woody shrubs (such as sumac) are abundant. ***Lesser adult bucks*** that remain off-range, feed on similar food-types in similar areas within their secluded ranges, and though having little contact with other deer, they make the switch from greens to browse at about the same time.

Identifying deer signs: whether deer are eating greens or browse, signs of a feeding area of a ***dominant buck*** (plus, possibly, one or more ***lesser adult bucks***), under the spell of airborne doe-in-estrus pheromone include 1) fresh, adult-buck-sized tracks and droppings (plus, possibly, slightly smaller tracks and droppings of one or more additional adult bucks), *the buck(s) dragging hoofs from track to track (clearly seen in snow)*, zigzagging tracks of individual bucks on and off trail, and 2) lots of smaller adult doe, yearling and fawn-sized tracks and droppings, fresh and old, zigzagging tracks of smaller individual deer on and off-trail. When feeding on browse, principle feeding areas of adult bucks or does and young are also characterized by abundant white tips (nipped-off stems) of woody browse plants inches to 5+ feet tall. Adult bucks visit principle feeding areas of individual does in estrus no longer than two days. *A four-star tip*: if the tracks of a hoof-dragging adult buck are not among smaller, equally fresh tracks, during feeding cycles over the next two days, that buck is almost certain to be found within the nearest principle feeding area of an adult doe (nearest to the site where the tracks are discovered). Signs of a feeding area of a ***lesser adult buck*** that has remained off-range include: 1) adult-buck-sized tracks and droppings, fresh and old, hoof-dragging absent or slight, zigzagging tracks on and near scrape trails in areas where few, if any, doe-sized tracks of any age are found, 2) fresh ground scrapes. (unlike dominant bucks, off-range lesser adult bucks commonly continue to renew scrapes during the primary breeding phase of the rut) and 3) where principle feeding areas exist, adult-buck-sized tracks and droppings, zigzagging tracks, mostly off-trail (few established deer trails exist in such areas).

Principle Feeding Area No. 4

Period: Nov. 18 – Dec. 1–15
Principle basis: rut phase IV
Principle food: browse.

Location: during the first week after the primary breeding phase of the rut ends, the principle feeding areas of *dominant bucks* will be the principle feeding areas of adult does nearest their buck bedding areas. Thereafter, if not pestered by hunters on foot, principle feeding areas of dominant bucks will be the largest and most secure browse areas in their ranges. Upon returning to former home ranges, some *lesser adult bucks* (and/or yearling bucks) will accompany suddenly-friendly dominant bucks for a week or so. Thereafter, all lesser adult bucks will key on principle, dominant-buck-like, feeding areas within their own home ranges most of the time, some bucks sharing principle feeding areas where located within overlapping sections of ranges.

Description: wherever located within their ranges, principle feeding (browse) areas of adult bucks are characterized by the following: 1) large size (wide patches the size of a football field or larger or long strips, 50 x 200 yards, for example), 2) dense screening cover (visibility at ground level often less than 50 yards), and 3) an adjacent escape area (a large wooded swamp, a steep and treacherous slope or posted land, for example). Though not a land feature, one other characteristic must be noted, generally the most important feature of them all: principle feeding areas (frequented long-term) of adult bucks are also characterized by no *apparent* hunters—none identified via sight, sound, airborne scent or fresh trail scent within 100–200 yards.

Identifying deer signs: signs of principle feeding areas of *dominant bucks* during the first week include: 1) tracks and droppings of one or more adult bucks, fresh and old, hoof-dragging absent or slight, zigzagging tracks, on and off trail, 2) lots of smaller adult doe, yearling and fawn-sized tracks and droppings, fresh and old, zigzagging tracks on and off-trail, and 3) abundant white tips (nipped-off stems) of woody browse plants inches to 5+ feet tall. Thereafter, signs of principle feeding areas of all adult bucks will be much the same except they may or may not include tracks and droppings of adult does, yearlings and fawns.

Principle Feeding Area No. 5

Period: Dec. 1–20
Principle basis: rut phase V
Principle food: browse.

Location: unless changes are forced by hunters, except during occasional two-day periods during which individual does are in estrus, adult bucks will continue to frequent principle feeding areas within their home ranges. Locations may change from time to time (generally because of hunting) and feeding areas may or may not be shared by other adult bucks and/or adult does with young. While in estrus, the nearest dominant buck plus a few or most other antlered bucks (including yearlings) living in the surrounding 1-2 square-mile area will be attracted to a late-breeding doe. Though only the dominant buck is likely to have the opportunity to breed, it and all other accompanying bucks will trail the doe to its principle feeding area during the usual hours for feeding. While feeding, the much-harried doe will move relatively fast and almost continuously, traveling a considerable distance throughout its feeding area.

After whitetails migrate to wintering areas, bucks feed among great numbers of other deer.

Description and Identifying deer signs: principle buck feeding area—same as described under "Principle Feeding Area No. 4"; principle doe feeding area—same as described under "Principle Feeding Area No. 3" (after whitetails switch to browse).

Post-Storm Feeding Areas

Whitetails can only smell airborne odors of hunters located upwind. Within the dense cover they so artfully use to avoid discovery, they often cannot see hunters more than fifty yards away. If it wasn't for their sensitive ears, they'd regularly be in desperate straits during hunting seasons. Ordinarily, wherever humans are located, whatever the wind direction and whatever the density of intervening cover, via hearing alone, whitetails can identify humans 100-200 yards away, pinpoint their locations, determine their directions of movements and thus endlessly maintain safe distances about them. When winds exceed 15 mph, steady or gusting, causing foliage and branches to rustle loudly, or when precipitation is moderate-to-heavy, raindrops, sleet or snow pattering loudly on everything, however, whitetails are seriously handicapped. They cannot hear hunters safe distances away. While such weather conditions exist during feeding hours, they dare not move from their beds. Whenever weather forces whitetails to forsake a morning feeding cycle, whatever the time of the day (unless within an hour or two of the usual beginning of the evening feeding cycle), within minutes after the troubling weather subsides, winds becoming light or calm, precipitation ending or becoming light, hungry whitetails rise eagerly from their beds and begin feeding. Such a feeding cycle is usually brief, lasting 1–2 hours, deer merely eating enough to subdue hunger until the evening feeding cycle. For this quick midday snack, deer will not travel far, generally feeding within or about the perimeters of their bedding areas or within the nearest definable feeding area.

While scouting therefore, make it a point to locate the feeding area, large or small (identified by the usual deer signs found in a feeding area) nearest the bedding area of an adult buck, and keep this site in mind when strong winds howl or moderate-to-heavy precipitation drums on the camp roof (to take proper advantage of it, you must be there at least thirty minutes before a local weather forecaster has predicted the wind or precipitation will end or become light).

Adult Buck Watering Spots

Whether attributable to innate aloofness or wariness, a sense of vulnerability while watering, the realization dreaded carnivores may lie in ambush near watering spots where there are great numbers of deer tracks (accompanied by more intense, accumulated deer scents) or the fact that dreaded carnivores also make use of many popular watering spots, adult bucks prefer watering spots rarely visited by other deer. As a rule, where deer tracks are abundant at water's edge, few, if any, will be adult-buck-sized. While scouting, therefore, always search for and measure tracks on trails leading to water, including isolated springs, favorites of loner adult bucks. Never ignore less-used deer trails leading to water. Wherever you find adult-buck-sized tracks, fresh and old, at water's edge, mark its location on your map. One day, you will take a buck there.

Trails Frequented by Adult Bucks

From time immemorial human hunters have keyed on the foot-wide, beaten paths made by sharp-hoofed white-tailed deer. Why? There are six basic reasons. First, deer trails are the most obvious of deer signs, the easiest to spot and the easiest to recognize. Second, whitetails live where deer trails are found; the more trails found, the more deer likely to be found. Third, whitetails are more apt to be encountered on deer trails, it being obvious they travel on deer trails much more often than in surrounding areas where there are no deer trails. It also being obvious they travel on some trails more than others, whitetails are most apt to be encountered on trails that are obviously used more than others. Fourth, deer trails make hunting easier, the footing generally less treacherous and less exhausting than elsewhere. Fifth, much-used deer trails provide relatively silent footing, improving the odds for encountering unsuspecting whitetails at short range. Sixth, deer trails reduce the risk of becoming lost, the hunter merely having to reverse direction to return unerringly to the starting place.

A buck like this has two rules: 1) never use the same trail twice in a row and 2) travel off-trail at least half of the time.

Whether deliberate or unwitting, the hunter who keys on deer trails for the above reasons is very unlikely to take an adult buck. Day in and day out, adult bucks make a mockery of every one of these reasons except the sixth (hunters manage that on their own). How? First reason: trails favored by adult bucks, largely loners, are rarely obvious. Most hunters ignore them and they are rarely identified (identified by measuring lengths of tracks and droppings). Second reason: older bucks tend to bed in areas where deer trails are few, commonly well outside of boundaries of adult doe home ranges where trails are characteristically abundant. They spend more than 90% of each day off-trail. Third reason: except while tending scrape routes (rut phase II), adult bucks do not often frequent heavily-trampled deer trails (trails characteristic of adult does and young). Of trails they do favor, they rarely use the same one twice in a row, routinely taking another of a dozen or more that are available each time an adult buck heads toward its principle feeding area, favorite watering spot or bedding area. Also, favored trails change each time feeding areas change. Moreover, particularly during hunting seasons, adult bucks travel off-trail at least 50% of the time. Fourth and fifth reasons: trails of adult does may make walking easier and quieter, but not trails of adult bucks. Wherever they go, adult bucks regularly pass through cover and terrain intended to disclose the presence of trailing predators or human hunters. Unless weather is favorable for stalking—winds strong and/or precipitation moderate-to-heavy—the average hunter walking along a buck trail is very unlikely to succeed in stalking near enough for an open shot at an adult buck.

Does this mean deer trails should be ignored while hunting adult bucks?

No indeed. Nine of the last ten adult bucks taken by my hunting partners and me were shot while there were using adult-buck-favored deer trails. Some were harvested via our "cover-all-bases" approach (see Chapter 2), developed specifically for hunting adult bucks that have proven to be especially difficult to ambush on any one trail.

It is not difficult to predict the current location or next destination of an adult buck, but to avoid alerting or alarming quarries, to keep them coming back where they are predictable and vulnerable, again and again, it is necessary to hunt these sites from afar and get to stand sites while quarries are yet 200 yards or more away. This generally means the hunter must key on adult-buck-favored deer trails. Though it is easy to determine exactly which trails are currently favored by adult bucks, it's never easy to predict which of them will be favored during the next half-day of hunting, i.e., never easy to predict with the necessary 10–50 yard accuracy.

There are at least five ways to improve the odds for making predictions with 10–50 yard accuracy (all of which will be explained in detail later in this chapter): 1) key on quarry-favored trails within 100–200 yards of their current locations or next destinations (whatever distance is appropriate under current circumstances), 2) key on quarry-favored trails within 100–200 yards of current locations or next destinations where cover, a lack of cover or terrain limits or concentrates buck movements, 3) key on quarry-favored, downwind approach trails and upwind departure trails, whichever is appropriate, 4) key quarry-favored trails coursing through very dense cover (cover that will be very dense after leaves have fallen) and 5) key on quarry-favored trails adjacent to escape areas.

As previously mentioned, trails that converge on or diverge from bedding and feeding areas of adult bucks are like the spokes of a bicycle wheel. As these spokes (trails) continue outward, becoming farther and farther apart, they begin to branch and cross spokes and branches projecting from other range elements. While traveling across middle areas where great numbers of spokes and branches cross, adult bucks have the greatest latitude for trail selection, making their routes least predictable in this section (the hunters odds for success generally 1–in–12 or less). While traveling within 100–200 yards of bedding and feeding areas (the nearest a hunter should approach) where branches are few and spokes are close together, adult bucks have the least latitude for trail selection, making their routes most predictable (the hunter's odds generally 1–in–6 to 1–in–4, sometimes better).

Upon departing from a current location, a feeding area, for example, an adult buck will generally begin by looping upwind, thus making certain it will not encounter an ambushing predator or human at short range. If the buck's bedding area is upwind, it will continue in that general direction. If downwind, it will either return via very dense cover, traveling cautiously off-trail, if necessary, halting frequently to listen and peer ahead, or it will will return via a trail bordering an escape haven, detouring widely, if necessary, ever ready to bolt to safety should a dangerous predator or man suddenly appear in its path. Upon nearing its destination, whatever direction it approaches from, it will loop to a downwind perimeter trail, stealthily studying the area via sight, sound and scent before moving in.

While scouting before the opener, therefore, always make it a point to circle bedding areas, current principle feeding areas and probable future principle feeding areas of selected quarries, inspecting adjoining 200-yard sections of all approach trails and perimeter trails (may be fragmented or not present at all), all potentially critical to future stand hunting success. Keep your eyes peeled for land features that may force lazy bucks to use certain trails daily—a steep promontory, a wet swamp, a beaver pond or a clearing that projects deeply across a buck's home or breeding range, for example, perhaps two of each projecting from opposite sides, forming a narrow passage. Always check out notches in high crests (saddle areas), shortest routes (deer trails) across bogs or bands of dense screening cover across openings. Land features won't change, and the effects they may have won't change. If your quarry is moving through or using such areas today, as long as it is not alerted or alarmed, it will continue moving through or using the same areas long after the opener. Above all, unless you have a darn good, tangible reason, never commit yourself to any section of deer trail, no matter how promising one may appear, unless it has the proven buck hunting value of those sections of trails listed above. With the exception of scrape trails, hunted during the proper period other sections will only break your heart.

Buck Scrape Trails

Fresh ground scrapes excite the imagination of whitetail hunters like no other deer sign, so much so that many hunters commit themselves to hunting ground scrapes, natural or artificial, during almost every period of fall and early winter. Before you fall into the same trap (if you haven't already), be aware of the fact that ground scrapes make lousy (unproductive) buck stand sites except during the period in which antlered bucks make and renew more than 90% of ground scrapes—rut phase II, the 2–3 week period *before* the primary breeding phase of the rut begins. If you plan to hunt during this period, you are justified in putting a lot of effort into hunting ground scrapes. During this period, adult buck bedding areas are the only sites likely to be as productive.

As I have explained in previous editions of the *Whitetail Hunter's*

Almanac, there are three classes of ground scrapes: those made by yearling bucks, those made by lesser adult (generally non-breeding) bucks and those made by dominant (breeding) bucks. Yearling bucks make few ground scrapes (generally located off-trail in feeding and bedding areas of their mothers), they are usually only about a foot in diameter and they are commonly found at the foot of yearling-type antler rubs—on trees an inch or less in diameter. Ground scrapes of adult bucks are generally two or more feet in diameter, most are located at traditional sites (the same spots, year after year), they are made along obvious deer trails, overhanging branches are mangled (especially during the final days before breeding begins), fallen leaves, turf and soil are pawed widely to one or more sides and they are regularly renewed. Features that differentiate scrapes of dominant bucks from those of lesser adult bucks include the following: 1) scrapes of dominant bucks are generally larger than those of lesser adult bucks, up to ten feet in diameter, 2) scrapes of dominant bucks are found within home ranges of does (areas characterized by dense networks of deer trails); those of lesser adult bucks (after being run off) in other areas (areas characterized by few deer trails), 3) scrapes of dominant bucks are generally found along major deer trails; scrapes of lesser adult bucks along minor deer trails; 4) dominant bucks generally mangle overhanging branches more and paw more leaves, turf and soil farther, commonly out to ten feet and dominant bucks renew ground scrapes more often, generally every 24–48 hours unless it is unseasonably warm or hunters are discovered near scrapes (which is almost routine).

The Johnny-on-the-spot approach is particularly effective for hunting adult bucks maintaining ground scrapes. If you plan to hunt adult bucks during this period, it is particularly important to be able to key on scrapes without alerting or alarming quarries. For reasons I cannot adequately explain, adult bucks, particularly dominant bucks, are especially sensitive during this phase of the rut. Likely stand sites must be located at least 2–3 weeks before bucks begin making ground scrapes. Since dominant and lesser adult bucks generally make most of their scrapes at the exact same sites as long as they live and succeeding dominant bucks generally adopt the exact same ground scrape sites used by their predecessors, stand sites selected near scrapes made during the previous fall will generally be as productive as stand sites selected after bucks have begun a new round of making ground scrapes. It really doesn't matter when you scout for scrapes, as long as it isn't during the period when bucks are making and renewing them—bucks likely to abandon scrapes where humans are discovered. As explained earlier, I personally prefer scouting for scrapes after snow-melt in spring. At that time scrapes appear as fresh as the day they were made and they are easier to spot than during any other period of the year. At other times, you almost have to know exactly where to look for them to find them.

Adult Doe Range Elements

A buck's main purpose in life is to breed. Though does only breed three months out of the year, practically everything a buck does year-around is directed toward breeding, including growing antlers, battling to the top of the local buck pecking order and making antler rubs and ground scrapes. Since hunting seasons generally fall during the period bucks are most intensely involved with breeding related activities, does play an irrevocable role in buck hunting. Knowing where certain adult bucks bed, feed and water is rarely enough to assure hunting success. While scouting, the hunter must also locate range elements of the female deer that will dominate the lives of intended quarries during the hunting season. Having much smaller home ranges and young that cannot outrun large predators until they are 60-90 days old, maternal does (adults and yearlings) utilize their separate ranges in a somewhat different fashion than adult bucks.

Adult Doe Bedding Areas

Bedding areas of adult does are particularly productive buck stand sites during rut phases III (the primary breeding phase) and V (the supplemental breeding phase). While does are in estrus, most breeding occurs midday in doe bedding areas. Does in heat are not inclined to bed lengthy periods, if at all. Closely trailed by the dominant buck and her young, and, perhaps, by one or more other bucks (including the doe's much-threatened yearling buck), a doe in estrus will typically wander randomly throughout its large bedding area from morning feeding cycle to evening feeding cycle, halting to allow breeding 4-6 times.

Adult does and their fawns and yearlings, prefer to bed in deep grasses, making their beds and bedding areas easy to identify.

To protect less-fleet young fawns from discovery by venison-eating predators (including bears, wolves, coyotes, foxes and domestic dogs), adult does use large bedding areas, 10-40 acres in size, and they rarely bed at the same site twice in a row, thus avoiding a build-up of predator-attracting fawn scents. Doe bedding areas are characterized by open patches of deep grasses among brush and timber. Deep grass makes excellent screening cover for small spotted fawns and the timber provides protection from wind, precipitation and the hot summer sun. Kept relatively scent-free, regularly licked by their attentive mothers, hunting predators would have to practically step on a fawn to find one frozen flat in deep grasses (freezing, lying flat, head down is an instinctive response of fawns upon seeing, hearing or smelling larger, unfamiliar creatures or upon hearing the warning snort of a maternal doe or yearling).

Because does and their young typically bed in deep grasses, their beds are easy to spot and accurately measure and their bedding areas are easy to identify. In Minnesota, beds of adult does and accompanying yearling bucks measure 40–42 inches in length. Yearling doe beds are generally about 38 inches long, fawn beds, 30–36 inches long (after September 1st). Beds are generally located off-trail, and fawn beds are generally located within a few yards of adult doe beds. Beds of yearlings may or may not be located near the beds of their mothers. Yearlings typically explore short distances off-range and feed and/or bed away from their mothers 25–50% of the time in fall, especially yearling bucks. Twin yearling bucks generally stick together. A single 42-inch bed found in deep grasses (no fawn bed nearby) is thus more than likely to be the bed of a yearling buck.

Like adult buck bedding areas, doe family bedding areas are also characterized by abundant off-trail droppings, fresh and old. In Minnesota, adult doe and yearling buck droppings average 1/2 inch in length, not including the nubbins at the ends. Like droppings of adult bucks, yearling buck droppings are commonly clumped (being soft) during fall and early winter. Yearling doe droppings average 3/8 inch in length, fawn droppings 1/4 inch.

Adult Doe Feeding Areas

Like adult bucks, maternal does favor certain feeding areas—principle feeding areas—but not uncommonly longer than six weeks. Like adult bucks, adult does also have at least two other "less-preferred" feeding areas they can readily use any time a principle feeding area is found to be unsafe.

Adult does do not seem to be as fearful of full exposure while feeding as adult bucks. This is doubtless due to the added protection provided by the extra sets of eyes, ears and noses of yearlings and fawns that accompany them while feeding, at least one deer having its head up, intently studying its surroundings, while the others contentedly feed. Fawns become very able rear-guard sentinels at an early age. For this reason, adult does and young tend to feed in more open areas (less screening cover), feed longer in more open areas, and feed farther from escape areas than adult bucks. While hunting is in progress, however, does and young soon begin using feeding areas exactly like those of more wary adult bucks, if not the same.

Adult does and young of surrounding home ranges also commonly share centrally located, off-range feeding areas—fields of favored farm crops, clearcuts rich with greens and browse and stands of mature white oaks dropping acorns, for example. In larger feeding areas family groups generally feed apart. Family groups may feed close to one another in smaller feeding areas, or in larger feeding areas where only small sections are considered safe—sections adjacent to dense woody cover most distant from roads frequented by poachers or in sections opposite from known stand sites of human hunters, for example.

Doe family feeding areas are characterized by lots of adult doe, fawn and yearling-sized tracks and droppings, off-trail.

Feeding areas of does with young are characterized by abundant adult-doe, yearling and fawn-sized tracks and droppings, fresh and old, on and off trail, zigzag trails of individual deer and occasional fawn-sized beds (30–36 inches in length). In Minnesota tracks of adult does are typically about 4-1/2 inches in length, tip-to-dewclaw (two-thirds that for hoof only—3 – 3-1/4 inches). Tracks of yearling bucks are generally the same in length, those of precocious bucks (destined to be dominant) up to 1/4-inch longer. Tracks of yearling does measure about 4 inches in length, tip-to-dewclaw, and tracks of fawns, 3 – 3-1/2 inches (lengths depending on whether fawns were born in May, June or July). While feeding on browse, doe family feeding areas are also characterized by abundant white, nipped-off tips of woody browse plants.

Large feeding areas rich with favored foods are likely to be shared by one or more adult bucks during 2–6 week periods, accounting for the the presence of adult-buck-sized tracks and droppings in some doe family feeding areas. Adult-buck-sized tracks and droppings may be attributable to regular visits by dominant bucks patrolling newly-established breeding ranges during rut phase II and breeding during rut phase III, one or more adult bucks accompanying does in estrus. Unless adult-buck-sized tracks and droppings, fresh and old, are found off-trail, tracks of individual bucks zigzagging, bucks making signs in doe feeding areas are merely passing through.

Adult Doe Watering Spots

Doe family watering spots, places where does in estrus will surely lead dominant bucks late in feeding cycles (after dark in the evening), are easy to spot and identify. The wet soil at waters edge will appear to have been thoroughly trampled by great numbers of whitetails. Generally, however, except in regions where accessible water is scarce, all tracks will measure 3 – 4-1/2 inches in length, tip-to-dewclaw.

Minimizing Changes in Adult Buck Range Utilization

Attributable to Hunting

Changes in range utilization attributable to Johnny-on-the-spot buck hunting cannot be avoided. Each time the hunter experiences an unsuccessful half-day of hunting, though the intended quarry may have passed unaware, out of range or out of sight, the hunter must always assume he or she was discovered and avoided, meaning, over the next week or more the buck will not approach within 100 yards or so of the site where the hunter was sitting. Each time a Johnny-on-the-spot buck hunter moves to a new stand site 100 yards away, the quarry will have 6.5 fewer acres (13 acres per day) in which to maintain normal, predictable habits within known range elements during normal, predictable hours. Each time the hunter moves to a new stand site 200 yards away, up to a 30-acre bite (up to 60 acres per day) will be taken out of the buck's home or breeding range. Inevitably (if not taken or seriously alarmed first), the buck will not have enough secure area remaining in which to maintain normal habits, forcing it to abandon its range or become completely nocturnal.

As you become familiar with an intended quarry's range, and hunting plans begin evolving in your mind, foremost in your thinking should be the desire to delay range abandonment as long as possible. The longer a quarry maintains normal, predictable habits, utilizing known range elements during predictable time periods, the better will be your odds for taking that buck, success most often merely a matter of time.

To insure there will be adequate time, plan to work slowly across a buck's range, taking small, stepwise bites out of areas currently frequented by the buck. This plan will not *always* be practical. Winds will change direction and natural forces will cause the buck to make changes in range utilization regardless of hunting, sometimes making it necessary to scout and hunt deep or distant range elements in a helter-skelter fashion regardless of risk. Generally, however, unless fresh buck signs and an effective stand site cannot be found within 150 yards inside the perimeter of a buck's home or breeding range, or within 150 yards of your last stand site, it should be your rule to give your quarry the largest secure area possible for as long as possible, never penetrating (or crossing) a currently secure area more deeply than 150 yards.

Locating Approaches to Mid-Hunt Scouting Areas

As important as knowing where to scout while hunting is knowing how to get there without alerting or alarming deer. Since I will cover mid-hunt scouting in great detail later in this chapter, at this point I will simply list basic guidelines for mid-hunt scouting. Wherever you find a trail or site likely to be frequented by your quarry during the hunting season, never depart without making certain you can stick to these guidelines while scouting or hunting, whatever the wind direction. If you find a potentially productive stand site where these guidelines cannot be fulfilled, or can only be fulfilled while the wind blows from a certain direction, forget the site or only scout or hunt there while the wind is favorable. Where stealth will be hampered by cover or terrain, conservative alterations are acceptable to within 75 yards of a potentially productive stand site (cutting paths through windfalls or dense cover or using windfalls to build side-by-side two-log bridges across mud or water, for example).

Heading into dense cover downwind of area to be scouted for fresh buck tracks.

Basic guidelines for mid-hunt scouting are as follows:

First, it should be your goal to approach no nearer than 200 yards of your quarry's likeliest current location.

Second, when a big buck is your intended quarry, *never* rely on anything claimed to cover (mask) or eliminate human odors. *Always* approach via a downwind area shaped like a quarter of a pie, the pointed end resting on a trail or site where you expect to find fresh deer signs made by your quarry.

Third, *never* fully expose your human form while moving on foot within 300 yards of the likeliest current location of a quarry. Within this distance *always* stick to cover or terrain that will reveal no more than mere brief glimpses of less than half of your moving body. No-glimpse cover or terrain is best. *Always* avoid openings and sky-lighting on open crests of ridges, hills, bluffs or mountains. *Always* wear a camo headnet and camo gloves, making certain no significant portions of your skin are exposed.

Fourth, *always* keep your eyes peeled for silent footing and fresh deer signs, not deer. Move steadily at a moderate pace, *never* halting except to measure deer signs, and then as briefly as possibly. *Never* move furtively (as if sneaking), halting often to peer about and listen.

Fifth, *never* scout any farther than necessary. Upon discovering the first fresh tracks or droppings of an adult buck within 200 yards of an area likely to be frequented by your quarry (right now), stop. Advancing no farther, visually or mentally (recalling one found before the opener) select an effective stand site within easy shooting range of those fresh signs. Then hunt (sit) or depart via your approach route, moving in the same manner.

Locating Probable Stand Sites and Approaches

As it's typically done, selecting one or more stand sites weeks or months before the opener is like playing poker without being allowed to look at the cards—all the hunter can do is put his money on the table and hope for the best. When playing against pros like adult bucks, the odds of winning faces-down poker are only about 1-in-30.

The Johnny-on-the-spot buck hunter plays a different game. He deals himself as many cards (stand sites) as he wants—thirty, forty, fifty; more, if that suits him. There's no limit. With the exception of one card— the opening morning stand site— the hunter makes no play until he looks at the cards, betting on none but the best. That's one of the beauties of Johnny-on-the-spot buck hunting: selecting as many stand sites as you want, and then, based on circumstances at the moment (the presence of very fresh deer signs made by an intended quarry), using only the best. Theoretically, the hunter should win almost every time, but adult bucks are canny at this game. They usually have an ace or two

Checking natural shooting windows in cover at a probable future stand site.

up their sleeves, but even when they don't, it's tough to keep them from folding and calling it quits, at least until the next feeding cycle begins.

Back in the old days, I combined stand site preparation with scouting (like most stand hunters still do today). Though portable stands made it easier, at best, I could only find and prepare 3–4 stands per day. With up to seven hunting partners putting dibbs on stand sites, I rarely began a hunting season prepared to hunt all locations I personally considered "most promising." Much to my usual dissatisfaction, I never had enough time or enough portables to cover everything.

Today, I can easily find and fully prepare as many as fifty stand sites in a single day, maybe more. The reason is, I hunt at ground level only, utilizing natural screening cover. For this, I need only one portable stand—the silent, camo-colored, folding stool I tote on my back—and I do absolutely nothing to prepare a stand site. While scouting, all I have to do is place my stool on the ground within easy shooting range of the trail or site where I am likely to see a buck during the hunting season, briefly sit on the stool to make certain I will have adequate screening cover and a natural shooting window to the spot where I expect to shoot the buck, and mark the spot on my map.

If an adult buck happens to pass the site later, other than noting my trail scent (which will persist 24–48 hours), it will discover absolutely nothing there even remotely suggestive of a human ambush site. Nothing will induce the buck to begin regularly detouring around the site—the usual response of most adult bucks today upon discovering a newly prepared stand site.

Curiously, not all whitetails readily recognize signs of human ambush. Whereas many adult does are altogether adult-buck-like in this regard, fawns and yearlings not under the leadership and direction of older deer (alone) are unlikely to identify and begin avoiding stand sites until they have actually encountered and identified humans at such sites. The greater sensitivity of adult deer is apparently developed (learned) over a period two or more years, either via associating with older, more dominant deer, submitting to their direction and leadership as younger whitetails are wont to do, as a result of surviving fearsome encounters with humans at such sites, or both. Like children of gifted human athletes, fawns of an area where adult deer have a well developed sensitivity to signs of human ambush sites seem to develop the this sensitivity more rapidly that fawns of other areas, suggesting of some kind of genetic disposition for greater sensitivity (a theory arising from noting marked differences in stand site sensitivity among adult deer in different long-term study areas). Since deer that lack such sensitively are more easily cropped by stand hunters, it stands to reason more and more surviving deer are deer with greater sensitivity toward signs of human ambush. Whatever genetics might be involved, it also stands to reason adult whitetails everywhere will become increasingly sensitive to signs of human ambush sites, inevitably forcing stand hunters to seek new hunting methods.

Why such sensitivity is most pronounced in adult bucks is yet somewhat of a mystery to me. Being loners from age two likely has a great deal to do with it. Not being protected by multiple sets of eyes, ears and noses like deer of doe family units (small herds), adult bucks must be more alert, observant and cautious than other deer as they move about their ranges. This by itself would make them more conscious of sights, sounds and odors associated with hunters using elevated stands; make them more suspicious of objects or changes characteristic of typical human ambush sites.

Over the past twenty-five years, I have spent an enormous amount of time observing or hunting whitetails while seated in tree stands 6–55 feet above the ground, up to 4000 hours during some years. Many deer known during those years became tame in my presence, opening the door to various kinds of testing. Early on, I rarely went to a tree stand without carrying a sealed container filled with some odoriferous substance characteristic of human hunters. While deer contentedly fed, bedded or moved slowly before me at various ranges downwind, I unsealed and released an odor into the air—the odor of toothpaste or another human's much-worn sock, for example. In time I not only discovered whitetails react with various stages of alarm upon discovering more than 100 odors characteristic of humans, but they can smell these odors at ground level 25–50 yards downwind, the area in which they could smell these odors becoming increasingly wider area as the downwind range increases. It thus became obvious airborne human odors not only spread out horizontally as they waft downwind, but they spread out vertically as well, filling an ever-enlarging cone-shaped space that touches the ground 25–50 yards downwind. This discovery meant, of course, contrary to popular belief, whitetails more than 25–50 yards downwind can readily smell hunters in tree stands, whatever their height.

Similarly, I tested various sounds typical of tree stand hunters—hammering, sawing, chain rattling, dropping branches, squeaking boot soles, rubbing tree bark and such.

Next, I turned my attention to determining what adult deer recognize visually as signs of human ambush sites (tracks in snow revealing responses to various tests). Much to my surprise, the dominant bucks of my far-north study area readily spotted everything from more obvious stand platforms, ladders and sawn branches to less obvious screw-in tree steps and the white tips of brush in cleared shooting lanes. Wondering if they were capable of spotting more subtle changes, I began tying a mere three-inch ribbon to trailside branches. Every dominant buck in the area spotted that ribbon from a range of 30–50 yards, backed away and detoured around it.

Realizing the human form is a distinctive visual part of a tree stand in operation, I next turned to testing designed to determine what makes the human body visually recognizable to whitetails. The most important of what I discovered was whitetails cannot easily identify a human unless the human's head is clearly visible (eyes, ears and skin visible) and/or the human is upright (standing).

These discoveries plus subsequent observations of my hunting partners in tree stands led me to realize the futility of using tree stands to observe or hunt the adult bucks of my wolf country study area. No matter what we tried, no matter what camouflage clothing we wore, adult bucks continued to identify and avoid our elevated stands from the day they were prepared.

A state of the art permanent tree stand—loaded with visual changes readily recognized by today's adult bucks.

The reasons were obvious. We could never completely eliminate sky-lighting. Even amongst dense branches of evergreens, photographs revealed our dark forms and platforms were large, very unnatural masses starkly silhouetted against bright skies, obviously visible over considerable distances. While standing, our silhouettes could not be mistaken for that of any other creature known to whitetails.

Also, the trees we used became distinctly different in appearance, eye-catchers over considerable distances. Try as we did, unnatural alterations could not be avoided. Our platforms could not be put into trees that provided any acceptable measure of screening cover without sawing away at least a few branches, producing noticeable notches in the cover and light-colored eye-grabbing axe and saw cuts at platform level; also loose branches strewn about the bases of our trees. We could not climb silently to platforms in such trees (a prerequisite to hunting success) without sawing away additional branches at buck eye-level lower down. Also, of course, we had to install means of climbing—totally-unnatural, screw-in or strap-on steps or ladders.

One day I sat down to make a list of changes I could see at a newly prepared stand site. By the time I was done, I had listed more than thirty very obvious changes, and many more that were not so obvious. "Chances are," I concluded, "the first adult buck that sees this stand site could double the length of this list."

The way I figured it, we had no choice but to begin hunting bucks at ground level. Sitting at ground level (using portable stools), wearing camo headnets, hiding ourselves within natural, untouched, downwind cover and utilizing natural, unaltered shooting windows (no prepared shooting lanes), *we found we could completely eliminate every single handicap imposed by tree stands.* No longer easy to identify via sight, sound or scent, unsuspecting adult bucks began approaching within 10–50 yards with startling regularity.

The first time my boys and I began scouting in anticipation of Johnny-on-the-spot buck hunting, after twenty-some years of tree stand hunting, we could not shake the feeling something was amiss. "With no tree stands to prepare," we kept saying, "scouting seems too easy. It's almost like cheating." As one of my sons later noted, however, "Good trees for tree stands are hard to find at the right spots, but good spots to sit on a stool are almost everywhere. Now I can hunt a lot of places I wanted to hunt before but couldn't because good stand trees were not available there." Now that such scouting is second-nature to us, wherever we pause to measure buck tracks or droppings, our eyes automatically scan our surroundings for adult-buck-effective, ground-level stand sites.

An adult-buck-effective stand site is a stand site with the following six characteristics: 1) natural, *skyless* cover in back—tree trunks, branches, brush, windfalls, foliage of any kind, rocks, boulders or a steep slope or bank—2) natural, shoulder-height-while-sitting, silhouette-and-motion-hiding screening cover in front, not altered in any way, 3) a trail, scrape trail or site currently frequented by an adult buck (as revealed by very fresh deer signs) 10–50 yards upwind, 4) a currently frequented bedding area, feeding area or watering spot 100–200 yards away, 5) one or more natural, sitting-level shooting windows to the trail or site frequented by the quarry (all shooting done from a sitting position), not altered in any way, and 6) accessible via 100–200 yards of man-tall-plus screening cover and/or screening terrain downwind.

While scouting for places to scout or hunt during the hunting season, wind direction must be a constant consideration. While on the move, you can stick to heavy cover, and while hunting, you can sit still and wear a camo headnet, fairly well eliminating the likelihood of being visually recognized by a buck. You can avoid talking out loud, sneezing, coughing and nose–blowing and watch your step, fairly well eliminating the likelihood of being recognized by hearing. You can bathe your body and wash your clothing with scentless soap, avoid the use of odoriferous substances such as toothpaste and deodorant and you can avoid contaminating your body and clothing with food (cooking) and tobacco odors, but you cannot long subdue, if at all, the unique and distinctive odors produced by the billions of living cells and bacteria collectively known your human body. Wherever you go, your body odors continuously mingle throughout a pie-shaped area downwind, the line of the wind direction down its exact center. Because whitetails do not generally react to human odors originating from sources more than 200 yards upwind, this unshakable albatross, up to 90-compass-degrees wide (widest in light breezes), extends 200 yards downwind and is 314 yards wide around the curve at its farthest end. Whether you inadvertently position this quarter-pie-shaped area over an adult whitetail's current location or an adult whitetail subsequently walks into it, within moments that deer will know exactly what you are, where you are and what you are doing—moving nearer, moving away, moving right or left or not moving at all. Particularly while scouting or hunting alone, you must be constantly aware of where your pie-shaped area of airborne odor lies. You must constantly strive to make certain it does not sweep across your quarry's current location, does not blanket its next destination or does not lie across any portion of the path it will use within 200 yards of your stand site (detailed instructions provided under the subtitle, "Your Initial Half-Day Hunt").

The trouble is, while scouting two or three weeks before the opener, it is impossible to predict which direction the wind will blow on any one day of the hunting season, in turn making it impossible to make plans intended to insure quarries will not be alerted or alarmed by your unsuppressable quarter-pie-shaped area of airborne odors. West winds (southwest-to-northwest) may be most common, but during fall and early winter, weather is often so volatile that you are likely to wake to a different wind direction every morning. Thus, in addition to likely changes in range utilization, likely changes in wind direction compound the need to delay stand site selection until the final hours before beginning any half-day of hunting. To make certain you will be free to use the best possible stand sites during best possible periods half-day after half-day regardless of wind direction, wherever you find one likely stand site, always take time to find 1–4 additional stand sites appropriate to different wind directions. At the very least, select at least two (and appropriate approach routes), on opposite sides of any trail or site likely to be frequented by your quarry. Believe me, this precaution is worth the time and effort. When you're certain you're going to take a big buck at a specific stand site in the morning and a wind crosses you up, there is nothing quite as frustrating as stumbling around in the dark before first light, risking ruinous alarm, trying to find the acceptable alternate site you neglected to find earlier.

Upon finding a likely stand site, it is advisable to mark its location on a map of your hunting area, using an "X" for the stand site and a dotted line for its approach route. Next to each "X," add a notation indicating which wind direction will be most ideal for the site. At most stand sites, winds will be ideal throughout a 90-degree arc of the compass—from N to W, for example—your stand site and approach route lying in the opposite 90-degree arc of the compass—in this case S to E of the trail or site where you expect to spot your quarry. Map notations such as this, plus daily local weather forecasts, will keep you from making serious errors regarding wind direction throughout your hunt.

To determine which 90-degree arc of wind is ideal, you have to visualize the position of the quarter-pie-shaped downwind area in which whitetails will identify you via your airborne odors (also trail scent). Within 200 yards of your stand site, as long as this tainted area does not lie across a trail or site likely to be used by your quarry, as the following diagram illustrates, you can actually sit within 10-50 yards of a trail coursing from downwind without being smelled by your quarry—*the trick that enables you to hunt downwind approaches to bedding and feeding areas.*

Realizing how difficult it is to visualize the position of the quarter-pie-shaped area tainted by personal airborne odors, and knowing how important it is to be able to do this accurately, I have created a simple device that makes it easy—Dr. Ken Nordberg's Stand Site Locator© (pictured). With your back toward the wind, the "wind" arrow pointed directly downwind, this device will show you exactly where your airborne scent is going, or not going. Before heading to a stand site, whether intending to scout or hunt, this device, in conjunction with your map and compass, will tell you if it is safe to use

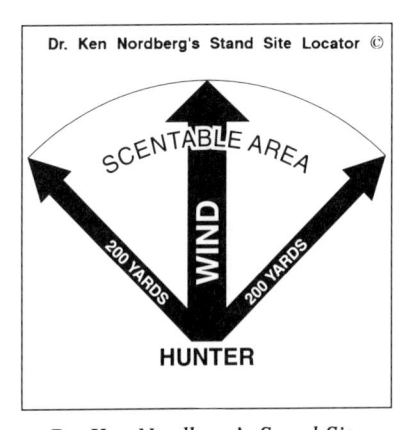

Dr. Ken Nordberg's Stand Site Locator©

the approach route you had in mind, and if not, the approach route you should use instead.

A full-sized version of my stand site locator is provided for your use on the last page of this book. After carefully removing this page and cutting around the outer margin, I recommend having your locator laminated at a local print shop.

While scouting before the opener, find all the likely stand sites you want, but at this point do not commit yourself to more than one—your opening morning stand site. Regardless of how inviting any stand sites may be, do not make the mistake of planning to use any until you have made sure your intended quarry has used the nearby trail or visited the nearby site during the previous 6–24 hours, and, of course, the wind direction is favorable.

Selecting a Stand Site for Opening Morning

When scouting two or three weeks before the opener, it is best to delay selecting an opening morning stand site until scouting is completed. At this point you will probably have several promising spots to choose from. Before settling on one, however, two questions must be answered: 1) will the buck currently frequenting the adjacent trail or site frequent the same trail or site opening morning and 2) will using this stand site have a negative effect on other stand sites used during subsequent half-days of hunting?

When an adult buck is the quarry, except during the month of September, a "yes" answer is practically a "gimme" for the first question. Sad to say, stand sites that appear especially promising now are unlikely to be as promising, if at all, opening morning. To determine where you should hunt instead, you should sit down, study your map and put together what you have learned via scouting and what you know about the future activities of the buck(s) you intend to hunt. Other than day-to-day effects of weather, which you cannot predict until weather actually materializes, the only changes in range utilization likely to occur will be those caused by changes in available foods and changes in activities characteristic of rut phases.

If you do not know when whitetails in your hunting area will make the big switch to browse, a date that tends to coincide with the first heavy snowfall of winter in northern states, and if you plan to hunt in November, make it a point to check browse areas for fresh signs of feeding daily while hunting (via mid-hunt scouting).

To anticipate changes in range utilization attributable to the five phases of the rut, you must know when each phase normally begins in your hunting area. Because dates for the onset of each phase differ from region to region, I cannot provide you with exact dates for your hunting area. I can, however, provide you with guidelines that will enable you to establish such dates with fair accuracy (plus or minus a few days) on your own. Personal observations during the coming hunting season will enable you to zero-in on these important dates. Because the onset of the primary breeding phase of the rut (the period during which about 85% of does are bred) is generally known everywhere, the following list of rut phases begins with this phase. Working backward and forward, a calendar at hand, you can then establish the approximate dates for the onset each of the other four rut phases. If you do not know when primary breeding begins in your hunting area, you can usually obtain such information by calling a state deer biologist. Do not settle for a date for the so-called "peak of the rut," whatever that means (a dubious term). Ask for the date breeding begins. If for some reason you are unable to obtain this date, this year, at least, you'll have to wait until fresh deer signs and/or deer sightings indicate when breeding has started. The day does begin experiencing estrus, dominant bucks will quit renewing ground scrapes, adult bucks accompanying does in estrus will begin dragging their hoofs from track to track and adult bucks will be seen closely trailing does during all hours of the day. For descriptions of activities of adult bucks during each rut phase, see "Likeliest Current Locations and Next Destinations of Adult Bucks," Key to Abbreviations (page 36).

Rut phase III, the primary breeding phase—from date of onset, usually lasts two weeks. Beginning date:_____; ending date:_____.

Rut phase II, the breeding range establishment phase—begins 2–3 weeks before the onset of primary breeding phase. Beginning date:_____; ending date:_____.

Rut Phase I, the development phase—begins the day antlered bucks begin shedding velvet, generally in late August or early September, and ends 2–3 weeks before the onset of the primary breeding phase. Beginning date:_____; ending date:_____.

Rut Phase IV, the recovery phase—begins two weeks after the onset of the primary breeding phase and ends the day does not bred during the primary breeding phase again begin to experience estrus, generally 2–4 weeks later. Beginning date:_____; ending date:_____.

Rut Phase V, the supplemental breeding phase—begins 4–6 weeks after the onset of the primary breeding phase and ends 4–6 weeks later. Beginning date:_____; ending date:_____.

Upon determining what adult bucks will be up to on the opener, don't be surprised (or discouraged) if you find you must do some additional scouting—search for more ground scrapes and more doe family bedding and feeding areas, for example. Later on, you'll be glad you did.

The second question above reflects the best odds for taking an adult buck on opening morning. Whereas the Johnny on the spot approach is very likely to put you within 50 yards of one or more whitetails almost every opening morning, under the best of circumstances it is unrealistic to expect to have the opportunity to take a 2-1/2 year-old buck during more than one of two opening mornings; a 3-1/2 – 6-1/2 year-old buck during more one of four opening mornings. Most seasons, you should not expect success until you have hunted 2–4 or more days, using 4–8 or more stand sites. With this reality in mind, your opening morning stand site should be the best, the most promising, the most likely to be productive, but its use should not jeopardize the effectiveness of other promising stand sites.

Unless you expect serious competition from other hunters, your hunting time is very short, you are willing to settle for "one good chance" to take a certain buck and/or you have 1–2 equally desirable bucks to turn to, do not begin a hunting season by hunting deep within the home or breeding range of an adult buck. The farther you travel on foot within the area frequented by your quarry during the pre-dawn period before the hunting season officially begins, a period during which the buck will be on the move, the more likely it is you will approach or pass within 100–200 yards, thus alerting or alarming your quarry. If you penetrate more than half-way across the buck's range during this period, alerting or alarming is almost certain. If you merely alert it, generally occurring without a hunter's knowledge, you will immediately create an area the buck will thereafter avoid during the hunting season—a circular area with a diameter of roughly 200 yards. Within this area the effectiveness of pre-selected stand sites will be ruined, of course, a fact that will become evident while mid-hunt scouting. If you should alarm your quarry, also generally occurring without a hunter's knowledge, the buck will abandon its range or become nocturnal, in either case becoming nearly impossible to hunt. Though deep stand sites are typically most tempting, it is best to begin by using the the most promising stand site located within 100 yards of the periphery of a selected quarry's range, thereafter making 100–150 yard advances, straight ahead or zigzagging into its range. Upon being identified by a quarry, this conservative, non-aggressive approach almost always results in alerting rather than alarming, in turn more or less insuring you will be able to hunt whatever number of half-days it usually takes, using whatever number of new (untainted) stand sites it usually takes, to at last meet an unsuspecting quarry at short range.

Because I hunt deep within a roadless wilderness, while selecting an opening morning stand site, I do not have to be concerned about other hunters. Most deer hunters, I realize, do not enjoy this luxury. If you limit your hunting to areas within one-half mile of roads or man-made trails, and/or if the area you hunt is normally hunted by others who wander on foot, hoping to "jump" a deer, you should expect the adult bucks of your hunting area to begin making dramatic changes in range utilization well before the first shot is fired, their next destinations being areas not often invaded by hunters on foot. If this is the situation where you hunt, your opening morning stand should either be located within dense woody cover adjoining an escape area on the far periphery of a buck home or breeding range or along a trail frequented by a suitable quarry within 200 yards of its bedding or principle feeding area (as explained earlier) one-half mile or more from roads or trails that provide access to hunters via motor vehicle. When necessary to hunt deep from the outset, trails to stand sites should not cross home or breeding ranges of intended quarry. One or more long, looping detours are part of the price you must pay to be regularly successful at taking adult bucks in regions where hunting is moderate-to-heavy.

Wherever you decide to begin, never settle for one stand site. Always select one or more alternate sites and approaches that will be appropriate for different wind directions. Never make it necessary to sit upwind of the trail or site where you expect to spot your quarry, wasting the "best" hours of a hunting season---those first few hours during which your quarry does not yet realize it is being hunted.

Having completed your all-important pre-season scouting, other than sharpening your marksmanship and putting together your hunting gear, you are now ready for opening day. Well, almost.

Step 2: The Opening Half-Day Hunt

Last-Minute Mini-Scouting

It has long been a Nordberg tradition to set up deer camp two or three days before the opener. After all the chores are done, including cutting, splitting and stacking a couple of cords of firewood, we rest up, play lots of cribbage and do a little last minute mini-scouting.

Midday, the day before the opener, we take brief, 1–2 hour hikes on trails along which we are fairly certain to find tracks and droppings of the bucks we plan to hunt. To minimize the risk of alerting or alarming our quarries, the moment we discover fresh adult-buck-sized tracks and droppings in the vicinities of our pre-selected stand sites we reverse direction and head back to camp. We move quietly and steadily at a moderate pace (like cruising wolves), heads pointed straight ahead, avoiding any display of hunting behavior and communicating only via hand signals (pointing and grinning, usually) and very soft whispers. Keeping downwind, we never approach within 200 yards of bedding areas, feeding areas and the stand sites we planned to use opening morning. Like mid-hunt scouting, this brief foray is primarily intended to make certain we will hunt within easy shooting range of trails and sites currently frequented by our intended quarries.

While scouting the day before the opner, we make do with what fresh deer signs indicate our quarries *seem to be doing*. For example, if a buck's very fresh tracks seem to lead toward a known buck feeding area, we assume that buck will be feeding in that feeding area as the sun peeks over the horizon the next morning. If the buck's tracks seem to be leading toward its known bedding area, we assume it will return to that bedding area sometime between 9AM and 11AM in the morning. If a dominant buck ground scrape has been renewed within the past 6–12 hours, we assume that buck will be renewing many of its other scrapes in the morning (while other deer are feeding). If one or two of its scrapes appear not to have been renewed within the past 24 hours, we assume the primary breeding phase of the rut has started, meaning adult bucks will be trailing does in estrus as they feed in their favorite feeding areas in the morning and adult bucks will not return to their usual bedding areas. If an adult buck dragged its hoofs from track to track, whether its tracks accompany the smaller tracks of a doe and its young or not, we assume that buck will be accompanying the doe it smelled—obviously located within 200 yards and obviously emitting doe-in-estrus pheromone—as it feeds within the nearest area where a doe and its young normally feed at this time of year. If we do not find fresh adult-buck-sized tracks or droppings in the vicinity of a pre-selected opening morning stand site, we assume it is proper to abandon that site in favor of a previously found stand site near a trail or site in the vicinity of the spot where fresh signs of a quarry *are* discovered at this time.

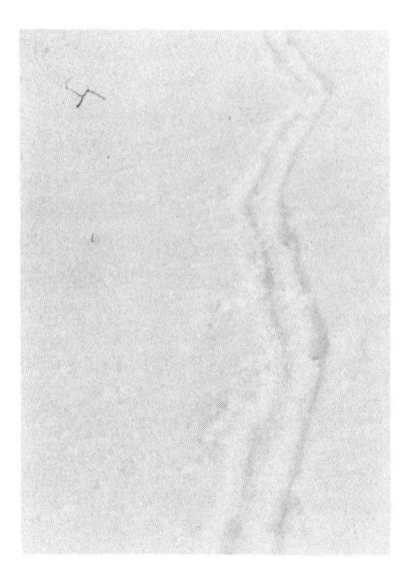

Railroad tracks—this buck will be with a doe in estrus in the nearest doe feeding area during the next one or two feeding cycles or in the nearest doe bedding area midday.

Over the years, we have taken many adult bucks because of last minute changes in plans attributable to our last-minute, pre-hunt, mini-scouting. This scouting has made it possible to pounce quickly (using portable stools) on dominant bucks while they are particularly predictable and vulnerable—while they are yet unaware they are being hunted and while accompanying does in estrus in known feeding and bedding areas during very predictable hours. As frequently bemoaned by members of our gang who do not arrive in camp until the evening before the opener, those of us who have the advantage of being able to scout briefly the day before the opener are most apt to take a buck on opening day.

Adjusting to Opening Morning Weather

As the zero-hour approaches, weather becomes a dominant subject in our deer camp, especially the direction of the wind. The portable radio, tuned to a local station, is turned on softly during the evening before the opener and during the pre-dawn hours as we hawk down our breakfasts. On our hunting map spread out on the table lies a compass and an arrow-shaped piece of wood indicating the current or forecasted direction of the wind. At least once each morning I step out of the tent, wet a finger and hold it high (the side becoming cool first indicating the current direction of the wind) to make sure our local wind direction is in agreement with the last weather report.

Sometimes, not often enough, the weather is perfect—the wind light and from the west or calm, the temperature normal for the season and a sunny or overcast day expected. Fog, mist or drizzle is considered "great!"

Whatever the weather, before we leave our camp, we're ready to deal with it, endure it, use it to our advantage. Whatever the wind direction, we know where we must go to approach our stand sites from downwind and where to sit so our quarries cannot smell us as they approach. Being portable stump hunters with a host of stand sites and approaches to choose from, we can readily adjust our positions at the very last minute, even as we draw near to the areas we originally planned to hunt.

Using a Stool for Whitetail Hunting

Over the past five years, while hunting and studying habits and behavior of wild whitetails (also wolves and black bears), I have come to regard the simple folding stool, shoulder straps and packsack attached, as the single most important piece of hunting gear a hunter can own and use. If I did not have mine on my back as I head out for a half-day of hunting, I'd feel vastly inferior as a hunter—a hunter very unlikely to take an adult buck.

If you have never used a stool while hunting whitetails, it might be difficult to believe such a contrivance could significantly improve hunting success.

You might imagine, for example, you could enjoy all of the same advantages by simply sitting on a handy stump, log or boulder. The trouble is, stumps, logs or boulders are rarely at perfect spots—hidden within adequate screening cover 10–50 yards downwind of a trail or site currently frequented by a suitable quarry. Moreover, stumps, logs and boulders tend to be wet, cold and/or uncomfortable to sit on. Most will force a hunter to move in less than an hour, just about the time an unseen buck that was 200 yards away is finally approaching. My stool gives me the freedom to make use of ideal stand sites almost anywhere, and it provides all the comfort I need to sit without squirming for a period of 4–6 hours, a half-day of hunting.

While seated at ground level, you might imagine you'd be a sitting duck when it comes to being spotted by approaching deer. Actually, as long as you wear a camo headnet (whether gun or bowhunting) and avoid staring directly at approaching deer, just the opposite is true. Never sky-lighted and ever hidden by the same kind of cover that so effectively hides whitetails, you will be astonished by how near whitetails will approach without exhibiting the least hint of recognition or alarm. While sitting without motion at ground level, a camo headnet covering your face (except eyes) under your cap, whitetails throughout the 270-degree arc upwind of where you are sitting will obviously have a devil of a time spotting and identifying you. While near, the biggest buck in your hunting areas may stare directly at you several times and still show no recognition or alarm. While standing on the ground or on an elevated platform (treestand), you will rarely see this happen. Today's adult bucks almost constantly search for and readily recognize the upright human silhouette both on the ground and in trees.

You might similarly imagine you'd be a sitting duck when it comes to being smelled by approaching deer. Again, just the opposite is true. Throughout a 90-degree arc up to 200 yards downwind whitetails will respond to your airborne odors exactly like they will respond to the airborne odors of a hunter at any height in a tree (from 25–50 yards downwind), but while using a portable stool, you will always be able to silently approach stand sites from downwind and you will always be able to silently place your stool on the ground, downwind of the trail or site frequented by your quarry (something a tree stand hunter can only do while the wind direction is favorable). For this simple reason, you will be far less likely to be smelled by an approaching buck. For that matter, because you will always be completely free to sit near trails and sites currently frequented by adult bucks (something hunters using permanent or noisy-to-tote-and-install portable tree stands can't do), a far greater number of adult bucks will find it impossible to smell you.

You might imagine you won't be able to see as far—a thought inordinately distressing to hunters accustomed to using treestands. This may be true. As a rule, however, whenever you can plainly see an adult buck at a great distance, it can plainly see you at a great distance as well. Back in the old days, it didn't matter; today, it does. Because today's adult bucks constantly scan trees for the dark silhouettes of human hunters, most find it relatively easy to avoid most stand hunters at great distances. While seated on the ground in the dense cover favored by adult bucks during hunting seasons, you will often find it difficult to spot approaching quarries until they are less than 50 yards away. I personally do not consider this to be a handicap. When you can't see a buck until it is less than fifty yards away, it can't see you until it is less than 50 yards away, in which case, it will not be able to avoid you until it is well within easy shooting range. I don't know what could be better than that. Having sat in tree stands 6-55 feet above the ground over a period of twenty-some years, up to 4000 hours in a single year, I admit I sometimes miss the greater field of vision provided by an elevated stand. This is probably why I lean toward stand sites located on natural elevations, hillsides overlooking spots where I expect to shoot a buck. If there are any advantages to sitting in a tree, the same advantages are gained by sitting at ground level on a natural elevation, including the greater field of view, but virtually all of the disadvantages of sitting in a tree are completely eliminated.

How to Make a Portable Stool Suitable for Whitetail Hunting

Now that I have succeeded in making you think you ought to buy a stool and use it this coming season, the first thing you'll discover is there aren't many, if any, available in sporting goods stores. Of those that are available, most have tubular aluminum legs. Tubular aluminum legs are too noisy for whitetail hunting, likely to make resounding metallic sounds whenever they contact, strike or brush against hard objects such as tree trunks. Such sounds are ruinous to hunting. Having worn out three acceptable stools in three years (somewhat pricy), I decided to make my own. Not only that, I decided to provide instructions for building a stool like mine for those of you who either cannot find a suitable stool or for the handymen among you who would like to build a good stool at a fraction of the cost of a less-durable or less-effective, ready-made stool. Here's how I did it:

List of Materials

1" (3/4" finished) x 10" straight-grain hardwood board 36" long

33 – 1-1/4" flathead woodscrews; 8 – 1-1/2" flathead woodscrews

2 – 3/4" flathead woo screws; 4 pop-rivets with washers

2 –1/4" bolts 2" long; 2 – 1/4" self-locking nuts; 9 – flat washers

1–1/2 yards soft camouflage fabric (for seat and packsack)

8'– 1" wide black nylon belting; 2 – 1" d-rings

26" – black nylon cord(drawstring)

Fabric cement

Flat camouflage paints

Step 1

From 1" x 10" board rip five 36" long pieces 1-1/2" wide.

Step 2

Cut into following lengths:
4 (legs) – 20-1/2"
2 (cross-pieces) – 14-!/2"
3 (cross-pieces) – 13"
1 (cross-piece) – 11-1/2"

Step 3

Cut 3/4" x 1-1/2" notches in one end of each 20-1/2" leg (as shown) and lightly sand rough edges.

Note: rough surfaces are preferred over smooth surfaces because they do not reflect light.

Step 4

Drill (countersink) holes for 1-1/4" screws. Make certain everything is square.

Step 5

Glue and screw cross-pieces to legs as shown. The outer (wider) set of legs has 14-1/2" long upper and lower cross-pieces. The inner set of legs has a 13" lower cross-piece and an 11" upper cross-piece. See photo accompanying step 7. The reason the upper pieces are assembled in this manner will become clear when the fabric seat is added. Use 1-1/2" screws when attaching 11" cross-piece (from sides).

Step 6

Drill holes for screws and attach upper-back cross-pieces as shown. Do not use glue. The upper-back cross-pieces for both sets of legs are 13" long.

Step 7

Drill 1/4" holes in exact centers of legs and insert 1/4" bolts, washers and self-locking nuts as shown. Each bolt has three washers—one on the outside, one between the legs and one on the inside. After your stool is completed (including painting), lubricate these bolts with Vaseline.

Step 8

Using a saw, cut off inner corners of lower ends of legs as shown.

Step 9

Saw, plane or sand down inner edges of upper cross-pieces as shown. This step will add immeasurably to comfort. When drilling and putting in screws, be sure to allow (save room) for this step.

Step 10

Apply several coats of flat camouflage paint. Dark colors such as olive and brown are best.

Step 11

To make a durable seat, fold a 29" x 18" piece of camouflage fabric as shown. The overlapping 1" seam is joined with fabric cement (dries in 20 minutes), forming a seat 13" x 18" in size.

Step 12

Adding fabric cement to the ends, the fabric seat is then screwed to place as shown. Use 7-8 1-1/4" screws to insure the fabric will not slip when weight is applied. Allow two days for drying before sitting on the stool.

Step 13

Fold a 6' length of 1" nylon belting in center and attach to stool with 1-1/4" flathead woodscrew and flat washer as shown. To avoid fraying, use a punch (rather than a drill) to make a hole (for the screw) through the belting.

Step 14

Place your stool (folded) on your back (the top about shoulder high) and place the straps (belting) over your shoulders. Mark each strap where it meets the bottom of each leg of the stool (nearest your back). Cut each strap where marked, melt cut edges with a match, fold about an inch underneath and attach ends to stool with 3/4" screws and flat washers as shown. Note: both ends of straps are attached to the same set of legs (see photo accompanying step 20).

Step 15

Cut camouflage fabric for packsack as shown. The front, back and sides are formed by the largest piece, 36" x 19". The bottom is formed by the smallest piece, 7" x 12". The top flap is formed by the remaining piece, 12" x 19", corners rounded at one end.

Step 16

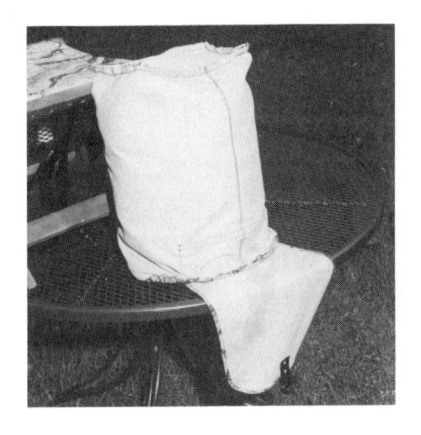

Sew fabric together as shown (inside-out). A wide hem with a bottonhole opening in front is made at the top of the bag to form a tube for the drawstring. After hemming the edges, the top flap is sewn to the center of the back of the bag 4" below the top edge.

Step 17

The 26" length of nylon cord is threaded through the top tube, ends tied together with a cinch knot. Burn the ends of the cord with a match to prevent fraying. An adjustable clip (optional) was added to the cord to keep the bag firmly closed while being toted afield.

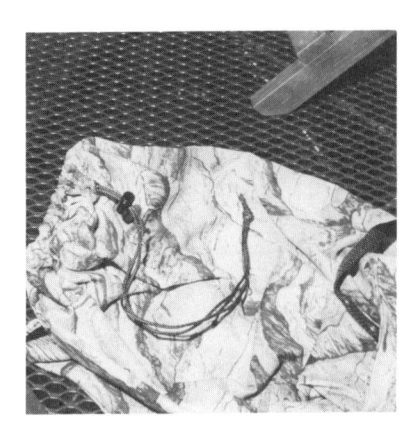

Step 18

As shown, a silent double D-ring closure is used to secure the top flap to the front of the bag. The D-rings are attached to the flap with a folded 6" length of belting, cemented and riveted to place. The 8" lower strap is cemented and riveted to a 3" section of belting on the inside of the bag.

Step 19

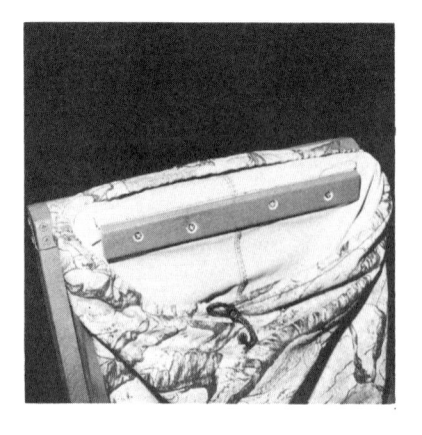

The bag is attached to the stool as shown. A 10-1/2" of wooden molding, 1" wide x 1/4" thick, is screwed to place with 4 - 1-1/4" screws inside the bag over the seam that attaches the top flap to the back of the bag.

Step 20

Following a little touching up with camouflage paints (rivets, etc.) and two weeks of backyard weathering, viola, the most important of my buck hunting tools— Dr. Ken Nordberg's Portable Hunting Stool ©— is ready to use.

The Perilous Journey to Your Stand Site

Before you know it, the first pink blush of the new day will appear on the eastern horizon, meaning it's time to head to your stand site. You've picked a dandy, and you have every right to feel the electric excitement that inflicts every hunter who knows a big buck will soon be near. But are you really ready? Will you conduct yourself properly along your stand trail? If you are a well-seasoned whitetail hunter, you might believe such questions do not apply to you. But they do. You're setting out to do something you never honestly thought you could do before. This is therefore different. It *has* to be different. If you started out doing what you are accustomed to doing, you'd be no more successful than you've been in the past. Though I fully understand what I must do when my quarry is a big buck, it's different for me as well. I must concentrate on what I'm doing all the way to my stand site and keep a tight rein on my thoughts. If I don't, I sometimes make the same stupid blunders I've been making for nearly fifty seasons (attributable to over-anxiousness).

Before starting out, let's make certain we are ready.

We've made ourselves as odor-free as possible, having used scentless soap on everything, our clothing and our bodies. We brushed our teeth with soda. We didn't wear our hunting clothes while cooking or smoking was in progress. However, before you go off half-cocked, thinking a deer can't smell you, sniff my hair and breath. Now sniff one of your own boots and the action of your firearm. They all smell, don't they. Any one of these odors will readily tell a buck you're a human. This is why buck hunting must always be "downwind hunting."

Now let's check ourselves for things that might make revealing sounds, especially metallic sounds. You and I may not hear it, but whenever two metallic objects loosely contact one another, keys, coins or bullets in a pocket or packsack, for example, while we are walking they will make identifying metallic jingles and rattles readily heard by whitetails 100–200 yards away. Either leave such things in camp or do whatever is necessary to make sure they don't loosely contact one another.

How about things easily seen? We've made sure our clothing does not reflect ultra-violet light, making them glow even in very low light. We either purchased outer clothing free of color brighteners or we've washed our outer clothing once or twice with soap free of color brighteners (and scent). We'll also don our camo face masks before leaving camp, thus making certain the bright skin of our faces and the distinguishing features of our human heads will not be seen by whitetails.

But what about our flashlights? Our eyes not being evolved for seeing well in the dark, we need to use flashlights. Once our eyes become accustomed to the dark, however, we'll be able to see quite a bit, enough to enable us to accurately follow long sections of our trails with no more than starlight, moonlight or northern lights to illuminate our paths, even if it is cloudy. Against the starlit sky, we'll be able to spot familiar landmarks over a considerable distance. It would be nice if our trails were marked with fluorescent tacks, but as I've recently come to realize, like the headlight of a railroad locomotive, which is designed to attract attention, the tacks force you to continuously swing your flashlight beam from side to side, horizontally. Considerable distances ahead, your flashlight beam will be extraordinarily eye-catching to whitetails. Older bucks, especially, fully understand what an approaching flashlight beam means. We must use our flashlights as little as possible, therefore, only using them when absolutely necessary and always carefully directing the beams down toward the ground. While moving toward a stand in pre-dawn darkness, never play the ruinous game of trying to locate whitetails via their glowing eyes.

All set? Let's go. We'll use the first 100 yards or so to get our eyes accustomed to the dark, get the kinks out our legs and get our blood flowing. To avoid alerting deer, from the moment we step outside, we'll communicate via very soft whispers only.

Now listen to your footsteps. Hear how loud they are? Hear the way your heels occasionally drag, making those scuffing noises? Such sounds, characteristic of human footsteps only, are easily distinguished by whitetails over a considerable distance. If they are frequently interrupted by periods of silence, they tell a whitetail you are hunting. If they are continuous, they tell a whitetail you are not hunting. To eliminate these sounds, bend your knees with each step. Hear the difference? Bending your knees forces you to pick up your feet and put them down lightly. Now you sound like a walking deer. It takes a day or two of conscious effort to become accustomed to walking in this manner. Until then, keep an ear tuned to the sounds of your footsteps.

Frequently stepping on branches that break loudly underfoot is also a characteristic of human footsteps. As you walk to your stand, it should be your goal to avoid stepping on branches that break loudly underfoot. In darkness, anytime you feel your foot come down on a branch or log, don't put your weight on it. Raise your foot and step over it. To do this, keep your mind on what your feet are doing, and don't move too fast.

Don't worry about sounds of leaves and grasses rustling underfoot. All large animals, including whitetails, make the same sounds while walking through leaves or grasses. As long as your footsteps are light and steady—no frequent pauses—and you do not drag your feet, whitetails that cannot identify you via sight or smell will not be able to identify you by your footsteps. They will likely mistake you for a passing deer.

Because we're wearing soft outer clothing, the swishing sounds we're now making as we walk through deep grasses and leafy branches are indistinguishable from the swishing sounds made by whitetails walking through the same grasses and leafy branches. If our outer clothing was stiff, hard and/or abrasive, we'd be hearing sounds akin to scratching on a window screen, easily heard and alarming to whitetails 100–200 yards away on calm mornings such as this. To avoid breaking branches suspended across your path, stoop under or go around them.

Our trails split near that big balsam up ahead.

The buck you'd like to take is now on the move, feeding. It began feeding a good two hours ago. According to what we learned from its signs, it should be feeding in the browse area that begins about 200 yards west of here.

You selected a stand site near the junction of two buck-frequented trails, one a perimeter trail, a bit less than 100 yards from the the northeast edge of the feeding area. Wisely, rather than attempting to hunt within or along the edge of the feeding area, intending to take the buck as it feeds, it is your intention to take this buck as it departs from the feeding area. It being dark and the buck being there right now, it would have been very foolish to attempt to move into the feeding area at this hour. If you blundered into that buck in the dark, not only would you have no chance of taking the buck, but in all likelihood it would abandon its range until the hunting season is over.

As forecasted, the breeze is from the northwest. You're okay there. You will approach from downwind, and as you noted on your map, your airborne odors should not blanket any portion of the two trails near your stand.

Your approach cover is dense. Nowhere will you cross a large opening and nowhere will you be sky-lighted, things to avoid even in darkness. If a whitetail is more than fifty yards away as you pass, it will be unlikely to identify you via sight.

All you'll have to do is concentrate on avoiding identifying sounds. If you don't sneeze, cough, blow your nose or break branches and if you tread lightly, moving straight to your stand site without stopping, you should be able to get there without being identified by your quarry; without alerting or alarming your quarry.

Your stand site is located near the center of a 200-yard-wide band linking the buck's current location and its next destination, its bedding area, the band curving somewhat around that swamp north of the feeding area. Within 100–200 yards of your stand, you will not cross either of the trails you will watch. Your screening cover is excellent and you didn't alter as much as a blade of grass. That buck cannot realize that spot is a human ambush site. You have two natural shooting windows that will enable you to fire from a sitting position. You should never stand up while a buck is within 50 yards. While seated, only your head will be fully exposed, but because you will be wearing a camo headnet, you won't have to worry about that. And you'll be as comfortable as you can be, able to lean back against a tree trunk and stretch out your legs. You should have no difficulty sitting without sound or detectable motion until 11AM.

Success vs Non-Success

If you are successful on opening morning, you will probably assume you did everything exactly right. Rightfully so.

If you are not successful, you might assume you did something wrong or what you did wasn't all that effective. While using the Johnny-on-the-spot approach, neither assumption is likely to be true. You can do everything exactly right, use the most effective of hunting methods and still not be successful. That's hunting. There are a host of possible reasons for failing to see a quarry where expected during any one half-day of Johnny-on-the-spot buck hunting, the innate alertness and cunning (intelligence) of the average adult buck, capricious weather and unexpected interference from other hunters among them. In most cases, however, a fruitless half-day of hunting is attributable to one of three factors: 1) the buck was somewhere else, 2) the buck passed within 100 yards but not within sight (perhaps within hearing, however) or 3) the buck identified you before you identified it, likely without your knowledge, and thus avoided approaching within sight or shooting range.

Logically, stand sites selected 2–3 weeks before the opener are somewhat plagued by the first factor. After midday scouting becomes a daily regime, the other two factors become dominant. Unfortunately, neither can be routinely eliminated, and when they are eliminated, the hunter can't realize it until a buck suddenly materializes at short range. Like curves, change-ups and fastballs keep the best baseball sluggers in the world from getting a hit every time at bat, these factors limit the number of half-days the best of hunters can be successful. Being able to make quick and effective adjustments daily (via scouting), you'll nonetheless maintain a fairly respectable batting average.

Step 3: Daily Scouting

As previously stated, Johnny-on-the-spot buck hunting derives its unusual effectiveness from keying quickly on very fresh deer signs made by selected quarries. Upon completing any unsuccessful half-day of hunting, this "very fresh deer sign" requirement makes it necessary to move 100 yards or more to a new stand site every half-day. Required fresh deer signs may be discovered while traveling to or from a previously selected stand site, eliminating the need for extra scouting, but it is usually necessary to devote 1–2 hours daily to searching for fresh signs and two new stand sites—one for evening today and another 100 yards or more away for tomorrow morning. This is done by cautiously probing 100–200 yards into one or more areas not previously hunted. It is the only way the hunter can be certain an intended quarry will be near during the next two half-days of hunting.

Scouting after the opener is vastly different than scouting before the opener. While scouting 2–3 weeks or more before the opener, it doesn't matter how a quarry may react to the presence of a scouting human. After the opener, alerting or alarming an adult buck is likely to be disastrous, immediately wiping out any advantage that might be gained by scouting, or worse, destroying any chance to take the buck during the balance of the

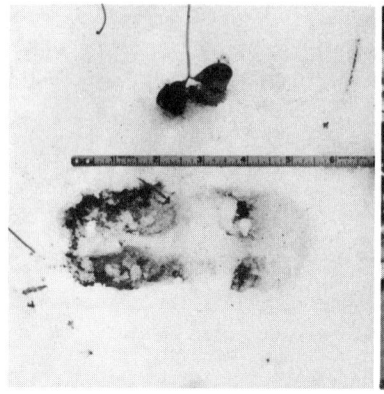

Just-made tracks of an unalarmed, adult buck...

or just-made droppings of a large buck—your quest.

hunting season. For this reason, blind or random groping is unacceptable while hunting. Mid-hunt scouting must be purposeful, specific scouting areas in mind before starting out. It must be cautious and conservative, and it cannot be a combination of scouting and hunting—still-hunting, stalking or trailing. While scouting, the hunter should be constantly prepared to take an intended quarry, should the opportunity present itself, but such an opportunity should not be expected or sought. Mid-hunt scouting should be pure scouting, nothing more, nothing less, every move planned and executed as if the quarry is standing or lying unseen 50–100 yards away, which at unexpected times may be the case.

There are only two ways to avoid alerting or alarming an adult buck while scouting: 1) approach no nearer than 200 yards—the easiest and safest way to do it—or 2) avoid being identified—always difficult. In either case, it is important to know your quarry's current location or, at least, its "most likely" current location, discovered via earlier scouting. Only then can you know when you are 200 yards away, downwind or effectively hidden by intervening cover or terrain. Only then can you know when it is critical to be extra stealthy.

Deliberately avoiding a quarry while scouting during a hunting season may seem somewhat ludicrous, particularly when you know where your quarry is and it is your intention to harvest that buck. To put things in proper perspective, remember the odds. While hunting on foot, whether scouting is a part of it or not, your odds for taking one adult buck per hunting season are only about 1-in-30. While using the Johnny-on-the-spot method, sitting near a trail or site currently frequented by an adult buck, though it may take 4–8 half-days of hunting to be successful, your odds for taking one adult buck per hunting season are practically 1-in-1. However tempting or however successful hunting on foot may have been for you during seasons past, never risk destroying 1-in-1 odds by hunting while scouting. Just find what you need to find and then hunt (sit) or get out of there.

When to Scout

To minimize the likelihood of alerting or alarming a quarry, mid-hunt scouting must be properly timed. Your basic plan should be to hunt (sit) while whitetails are moving and scout while whitetails are bedded. If you know where your quarry is bedding (a primary goal of pre-season scouting), and when, as long as you approach no nearer than 200 yards, travel

Hunt (sit) while... *whitetails are active.*

no further than absolutely necessary and maintain at least a moderate level of stealth, you can scout almost anywhere within the buck's range, including upwind of the buck's bedding area, without much risk of jeopardizing your odds for taking that buck. Therein lies a problem: from September 1st through December, weather and rut phases wreak havoc with the hours adult bucks bed, creating a quandary of sorts.

Moderate-to-heavy precipitation and/or a strong wind that begins more than two hours before sunrise will keep whitetails in their beds throughout the hours they normally feed in the morning. If the precipitation ends or becomes light and/or the wind becomes calm or light more than two hours before the evening feeding cycle is due to begin, whitetails everywhere will immediately begin feeding. Such a feeding cycle is usually short, lasting 1–2 hours, deer feeding in feeding areas nearest their bedding areas. If the wind is calm or light, a thaw, or near-thaw following two or more days of frigid weather (temperatures remaining below 20-above-zero) will also trigger a widespread (all deer feeding at the same time) 1–2 hour feeding cycle midday. The onset of such a feeding cycle is unpredictable, however, beginning any time between 11AM and 3PM.

Midday movements are also characteristic of certain phases of the rut. Only during phases I (September 1st through mid-to-late October) and IV (the 2–4 week period following the primary breeding phase of the rut) can adult bucks be trusted to spend midday hours, 11AM to 3–5PM, in their usual bedding areas.

During rut phase II, antler rubs and ground scrapes are usually made or renewed by adult bucks (dominant and lesser) during morning and evening feeding cycles. While weather is calm and cool and/or while precipitation

Scout while...   *whitetails are inactive.*

is light (foggy, misting or drizzling), such activity is likely to continue throughout midday, especially during the week preceding the primary breeding phase of the rut. While winds are strong (15+ mph), precipitation is moderate-to-heavy or the air temperature is unseasonably warm, adult bucks will bed midday, perhaps all day.

During rut phase III, lesser adult bucks that remain off-range (run off by dominant bucks during rut phase II) will usually bed midday. Dominant and lesser adult bucks accompanying does in estrus will be on the move from morning feeding cycle to evening feeding cycle, but only, usually, within the bounds of the 10–40 acre bedding areas of the does they're with.

During rut phase V, breeding occurs during two-day periods at unpredictable times. One or two weeks may pass without any breeding activity occurring at all. While late-breeding does are not in estrus, adult bucks regularly bed midday within their usual bedding areas.

The quandary is, should you hunt while bucks are active midday or should you scout?

If you know where to hunt while bucks are active midday, by all means hunt. Adult bucks are too predictable, both in time and location, and sometimes unusually vulnerable, especially while with does in estrus, to pass up midday hunting opportunities.

If you don't know where to hunt next—midday, this evening or tomorrow morning—then scout. If you don't scout under these circumstances, you are likely to waste your next 1-3 half-days of hunting, either sitting near trails or sites not currently frequented by your quarry or alerting or alarming that buck as you search for likely spots to sit. On days bucks are expected to be active midday, either scout during the hour or so before or after they are expected to be active, or scout while moving to or from your midday stand site, taking a cautious, 100-to-200-yard-deep swing through one or two areas not previously hunted as you go. If weather that normally triggers midday feeding is forecasted again tomorrow, upon quitting a midday feeding area stand site, search for another stand site 100 yards or more away near fresh adult-buck-sized tracks along a downwind trail leading to the same feeding area. If the required fresh signs are not found leading to or from the same feeding area, take a swing past another nearby feeding area.

Where to Scout

It is unrealistic to expect to take an adult buck every opening morning of every hunting season. Therefore, no season should begin without knowing where to scout for new stand sites daily. The goal of daily scouting during a hunting season is to locate stand sites likely to be in the path of an intended quarry without jeopardizing hunting success.

Areas to scout, i.e., areas that can be safely scouted, are defined by habits and behavior of adult bucks (not fawns, yearlings or does) that are aware they are being hunted by one or more humans. Following the initial half-day of a hunting season, an adult buck will be extra-alert to sights, sounds and scents characteristic of humans and extra-determined to avoid discovery, maintaining safe distances about humans. It will readily abandon the use of any trail or site within 100 yards of any spot where a human hunter has been identified. Upon finding it necessary to resort to rapid flight—having unexpectedly encountered a human displaying hunting behavior at short range, having been shot at or having been near when a firearm was discharged—upon discovering its normally secure bedding area has been invaded (or is frequented) by a human, or upon discovering it is no longer safe to satisfy daily needs or urges of the rut because too much of its home or breeding range is frequented by one or more humans, an adult buck will readily abandon its entire range 5–10 days or longer or become completely nocturnal, effectively eliminating any chance of taking that buck.

To take an adult buck, to create and maintain optimal odds for hunting success, the hunter must turn the tables. The hunter must become extra-alert to sights and sounds characteristic of adult bucks; extra-determined to avoid discovery and greatly alarming the quarry; ever intent upon ending up within 10–50 yards of its path.

A hunter wearing a camo headnet and sitting quietly without motion on a stool, downwind, can easily avoid discovery by the most alert of bucks located only 10–50 yards away. A hunter moving on foot, scouting, is unlikely to avoid discovery by the least alert of bucks 100–200 yards away. Daily scouting is nonetheless necessary. The hunter must find trails and sites currently frequented by the quarry within or about areas where the buck will spend more than 90% of its time during the next one or two half-days of hunting, namely, its currently frequented feeding area (the principle feeding area of a likely three), its bedding area and, perhaps, a buck-favored watering spot. Upon locating these range elements and trails favored by the quarry when traveling to and from these range elements, you have a formidable advantage—knowing exactly where that buck will be during very predictable hours. As long as the buck continues to use these same trails and range elements, during subsequent half-days of hunting your odds for taking that buck will continue to be be as great as they can be. Once gained, it should be your goal to keep this advantage as long as possible.

While scouting, then, though it will be necessary to approach within 10–50 yards of trails currently frequented by your quarry, you should make it a rule to avoid being seen or heard nearer than 100 yards downwind, or seen, heard or smelled within 200 yards upwind or crosswind of a quarry's regularly-frequented bedding area, currently-frequented feeding area or currently-frequented watering spot. In addition to airborne odors, your fresh trail scent should be found nowhere within these same distances of these areas. These distances, 100 and 200 yards, are the inner limits of the surrounding areas in which it will be relatively safe to scout during a hunting season. Since it should also be your goal to hunt (sit) as near as possible to currently-frequented range elements, it is generally unnecessary to scout much beyond these inner limits. For all practical purposes, then, you should limit your scouting to narrow, oval-shaped rings surrounding these range elements, retreating cautiously from the area as soon as one or two ideal stand sites are located near trails that were used by your quarry during the previous 6–24 hours. It being unnecessary to explore vast acreages, your scouting time and distance traveled will thus be minimal—a requirement of mid-hunt scouting when hunting adult bucks.

As when deciding when to scout, rut phases play a dominant role in determining where to scout. During rut phases I and IV, scout rings about bedding areas, feeding areas (greens during rut phase I, browse during rut phase IV) and watering spots of adult bucks (characterized by adult-buck-sized tracks and droppings). During rut phase II, scout rings about the same areas, plus scrape routes of adult bucks. During rut phase III, scout rings about feeding areas, bedding areas and watering spots of adult does, hunting along trails near those where one or more adult bucks have been (hoofs dragging) during the previous 6-24 hours. During rut phase V, scout rings about areas appropriate to both rut phases III and IV.

How to Scout

Scouting during the course of a hunting season is always challenging and potentially disastrous, but the benefits are great.

At least once or twice per hunting season, your intended quarry will be very near while you are scouting, not elsewhere as you thought it would be, and you won't be able to predict when it will happen. For this reason, you must approach every area to be scouted as if that buck is there. If you don't, you'll invariably end up kicking yourself during the entire following year, maybe many years. If you do, thus avoiding alerting or alarming your quarry, you might even be suddenly rewarded with an easy opportunity take this buck while scouting.

While scouting during a hunting season, you must constantly appear to be totally disinterested in whitetails (venison). You should never appear to be doing exactly what you are doing--searching for fresh deer signs. Whether identified via sight, sound or airborne scent, "searching-for-signs behavior" will invariably be treated as "extremely dangerous hunting behavior" by whitetails, avoidance of the area or range abandonment certain to follow. If identification occurs distant from your next stand site, simple avoidance may not jeopardize hunting success, but you won't be able predict where or when this will happen either.

As long as you remain 100 yards or more downwind and stick to dense screening cover or terrain that hides you from trails or sites likely to be currently frequented by your quarry, whitetails in the vicinity are unlikely to identify you as a hunting or non-hunting human via smell or sight. Aside from finding fresh signs of your quarry, your chief remaining concern, always, must be to avoid being identified via hearing. A favorable wind and dense cover can't hide your sounds. If you are identified as a hunting human via sounds, whitetails 100–200 yards away will treat you exactly as they would have if you were in

plain sight. If a whitetail is 50–100 yards away when it identifies you via sounds, it won't matter whether you are moving as if hunting or not. The deer will immediately begin avoiding you and the site where you were identified, or, if it is an older buck, it will likely abandon its range.

To avoid being identified via sounds, your eyes must constantly guide your feet. As long as you remain 100 yards or more from your quarry, do not often step on or push through branches that snap loudly ("never" is better), do not often stop and peer about as if searching for something ("never" is better) and keep your pace steady, footsteps light and unhurried, you will be unlikely to alert or alarm your quarry.

Because you can never be absolutely sure when or where you are a safe 100 yards or more away, you should never scout any farther than absolutely necessary. Upon approaching a likely site or trail, maintaining a safe distance of 100–200 yards from bedding and feeding areas, the very first fresh adult-buck-sized track (edges well-defined) or dropping (shiny) you spot is enough. This is all you need to be certain your quarry is currently frequenting the trail or bedding or feeding area ahead, upwind. This discovery plus an adult-buck-effective stand site within 10–50 yards are all you need to be certain you will be within 100 yards of your quarry during your next half-day of hunting. Unless you plan to begin hunting immediately, you should immediately back away, retracing your steps as cautiously as when you approached and maintain a distance of 200 yards or more from the site until it is time to begin hunting.

Be Prepared to Shoot

While scouting, keep your firearm or bow ready to fire at a moment's notice. You may spot your unsuspecting quarry moving past, perhaps approaching nearer, in which case you should immediately freeze where you are, standing, not moving a muscle (not preparing to fire) except while the buck's head is completely hidden by intervening cover or pointed straight away. More likely, you and your startled quarry will discover one another at the same moment, in which case your opportunity to fire will be very fleeting.

In either case, if you do not have an open shooting window, don't shoot. If you pass up a shot at an unsuspecting buck, you are almost certain to be rewarded with a better shooting opportunity later. If you pass up a shot at an alarmed buck, you'll probably meet again sooner or later, maybe sooner. If you shoot and miss, you may never see that buck again. If you shoot and lightly wound the buck, it is almost certain you will never see it again.

Caught by Surprise

You're scouting. Suddenly you spot a deer. It's frozen, starring directly at you, obviously ready to bolt. You react by freezing, starring back at the deer, trying to identify it. You are unprepared to fire or unable to fire because the range is too great, intervening cover is too dense to risk a shot or you sense any move on your part, raising you weapon, for example, will trigger tail-up alarm. Even if the deer is not your intended quarry, you are caught in a situation that may doom your hunt. If the deer bolts, bounding tail-up, snorting, and if your quarry is near and hears, smells (detects the ammonia-like danger scent released from the tarsal glands of a deer experiencing tail-up alarm) and/or sees the alarmed deer, it will immediately become similarly alarmed, the consequences as ruinous as they would have been if the frozen deer was your intended quarry.

What should you do?

First of all, you should not have stopped, froze and began starring directly at the deer. Before you halted, the deer was convinced you were unaware of its presence and merely passing through the area. Because you were displaying no hunting behavior, the deer was convinced it could merely freeze, wait until you had safely passed and then resume whatever it was doing. Your sudden halt, freezing and locking in on the deer with your eyes, all terribly intimidating acts to a whitetail, not only made it obvious you had discovered the deer, but obvious you had selected it as a prey. Your next discernable move will thus be considered a charge or a prelude to a charge, logically triggering rapid flight.

To successfully extricate yourself from this potentially disastrous situation, you must convince the deer you either didn't discover it after all and/or you have no interest in whitetails. The first thing to do is quit starring at the deer. Remaining frozen, slowly turn your head and eyes to one side, thereafter keeping track of the deer's actions via peripheral vision only. Within a minute or so the whitetail may settle down somewhat, convinced you no longer have an interest in it, whereupon it will flick its tail from side-to-side and begin moving slowly away. If it remains frozen, very slowly turn your entire body away from the deer. If after another minute or two it still doesn't move, begin walking away, slowly, steadily and quietly, never looking back (keep your fingers crossed). If you or the deer moves out of sight without the deer bounding or snorting, you have saved your hunt. The deer was only alerted, it is unlikely to do more than avoid the area where you met.

Step 4: A Succession of Half-Day Hunts

Opening morning, the only part of your hunt consigned to guesswork, albeit "educated guesswork," is now behind you. Though your intended quarry now doubtless realizes it is being hunted, you will now embark on a succession of half-day hunts, making optimal use of potent advantages provided by no other hunting method. *You will be the most difficult of human hunters for whitetails to identify and avoid, the least likely of human hunters to alert or alarm whitetails and you will have opportunities to take adult bucks because you will always hunt (sit) within 10–50 yards of trails or sites currently frequented by adult bucks.*

To make optimal use of these potent advantages, it is important to understand why they are potent advantages.

Until you have experienced it yourself, several times, it might be difficult to imagine an unsuspecting whitetail, much less a 10-point buck, standing or slowly moving, not showing the least hint of recognition or alarm, only 10–50 yards away from where you sit at ground level. Until you have experienced it yourself, several times, it might be difficult to imagine this scenario actually occurring three-times more often than when using any other hunting method, including treestand hunting. Nonetheless, it's true, and anyone can do it.

Other than a $7 camo headnet, a silent homemade stool with shoulder straps, scentless soap and a box of soda, no special gear, or skills, are needed.

To keep your personal odors to a minimum, always advisable when whitetails are within fifty yards, you must wash all your hunting clothing with laundry detergent free of scents and color brighteners (now available in most grocery stores) and hang everything outside to dry. Each morning, while hunting, you wash your body with scent-free soap, brush your teeth with soda and don a fresh set of underclothing.

Never putting your trust in products that are supposed to eliminate or cover (mask) your remaining odors, you always approach scouting areas and stand sites from downwind and you always place your stool where your airborne odors will not cross any trail or area currently frequented by your quarry within 200 yards of your stand. Most hunters, including tree stand hunters, are readily identified by adult deer throughout a surrounding circle having a radius of 200 yards, but the only deer that will readily identify you will be those that wander into your downwind scent vector, up to 90-degrees wide and 200 yards deep. Being much more concerned than most other hunters about wind direction and being completely free to make certain you are seated where your approaching quarry cannot smell you, you will be far less apt to be identified via airborne odors than most other hunters.

Camouflage clothing provides a bit of an edge, but even if you wear blue jeans, a plaid shirt, a blaze-orange jacket and cap and a camo headnet, you will be far less visible to whitetails 10–50 yards away than typical camo-clad bowhunters perched high in treestands. There are three reasons. First, your camo headnet (your cap worn over the top) eliminates the physical characteristics of the human head (including bright, hairless skin)—the first thing that enables whitetails to positively identify humans. Second, while seated, your human form becomes much less recognizable to whitetails. A seated human is also far less intimidating to whitetails, appearing to be at rest rather than hunting, as when upright. Third, your human form will be masked by "perfect" camouflage. Wherever you sit, your camouflage will always be faultless. Whitetails will never notice one thing different about it. They'll never shy from it. Sky-lighting will never be a problem. It's readily available almost everywhere, and it's *free*. It's "natural, unaltered, ground-level, cover," better known as "deep grass, a patch of leafy shrubs, small trees or dense brush, sagging tree branches or evergreen boughs, a windfall, a boulder, a hollow stump, a bank and/or a hole in the ground."

Whatever you do, never scout or hunt without a camo headnet on. Once you begin using a headnet (preferably one with a single, oblong eye-hole), and experience its obvious benefits, you'll soon be kicking yourself for not purchasing one earlier.

Unhampered by a safety strap, a small seat and a small, noisy platform (as when using a portable stand), you'll be able to lean back against a tree, stretch your legs as far as you want and otherwise enjoy the comforts of a wide, chair-high stool. Experiencing none of the physical punishment characteristic of tree stands, you will have little trouble sitting 3–5 hours without making readily discernable motions and sounds.

Upon doing all this, you'll soon be saying to the boys back in camp, "It's amazing how close they can come without seeing you."

Being difficult to identify, using a non-aggressive hunting style and deliberately creating an aura of harmlessness by avoiding hunting behavior while scouting and sitting quietly on a stool while hunting has an amazing effect on whitetails. These unique elements of Johnny-on-the-spot buck hunting very substantially reduce the likelihood of alarming quarries and other deer, in turn, substantially reducing the likelihood of range abandonment and/or becoming nocturnal. This means your intended quarry will remain within its range, maintaining normal, predictable habits during normal, predictable hours much longer than when using all but one other hunting method.

The exception is tree stand hunting. Once tree stand hunters are identified, however, generally occurring within the first feeding cycle of a hunting season, adult bucks can freely utilize stand-free portions of their ranges, living rather normally. Unable to move permanent stands or unable to move portable stands without making considerable noise, tree stand hunters are generally unable to adapt effectively to changes in range utilization characteristic of adult bucks during hunting seasons.

Such changes pose no problem to the Johnny-on-the-spot buck hunter. By scouting daily and striking while the iron is hot, keying immediately, that afternoon or the next morning on fresh signs made by an unalarmed quarry, the hunter and the hunted will rarely be a great distance apart. Within hours after a buck makes a change in range utilization, the Johnny-on-the-spot buck hunter will be hunting within the new area frequented by the buck. Within hours after a buck begins maintaining a distance of 100 yards about an identified stand site, the Johnny-on-the-spot buck hunter will be seated at a new site unknown to the buck, 100 yards or more from the site being avoided.

Around each spot where a hunter is identified, an adult buck will erect an invisible fence, a barrier it will not cross for many days, weeks or, perhaps, even years. Sometimes these fences guide a buck to the very spot the Johnny-on-the-the-spot buck hunter has chosen for a new stand site, 100 yards or more from the center of the fenced-off area. In this way, a half-day stand site will sometimes enhance the effectiveness of the next half-day stand site, and the next after that.

As effective as this hunting method is, some wise old bucks can make even a very skilled Johnny-on-the-spot buck hunter mumble disconsolately and stare blankly at a densely-scrawled hunting map at the end of quite a few half-days of hunting. Sometimes time simply runs out. Given adequate time, however, no buck can endlessly avoid a short-range encounter with a Johnny-on-the-spot buck hunter.

That's Johnny-on-the-spot buck hunting.

A spot of blood, the first in 25 yards. The buck was moving well, showing no signs of weakening. And it was in complete command of its senses, using every trick in the book to discourage pursuit. It knew we were on its trail. It had watched us pass twice. But we wouldn't give up. Catching up with this wounded quarry was our job; our obligation. We had to bring this hunt to a proper conclusion. The problem was, it was beginning to snow.

Chapter 2

On the Trail of a Wounded Buck

Johnny-on-the-Spot Buck Hunting and Some Important Hunting Lessons
[First published in condensed form in the February, 1994 Edition of *MidWest Outdoors* under the title, "The Learning Trail"]

My oldest son, John, shoots a Marlin lever-action carbine chambered for .44 Magnum. I bought this gun for him in 1974. He was thirteen years old then. I figured such a gun would be easy for him to handle and, judging by ballistic tables, adequate for hunting whitetails, at least within the 50-yard range at which we Nordbergs usually shoot our deer. Though John has enjoyed great hunting success over the years, the performance of his little .44 Magnum carbine has not always been exactly praiseworthy. Besides jamming now and then, that rifle has occasionally made it necessary to spend many difficult hours on trails of wounded bucks. It happened again this past fall.

It began with intensive scouting three weeks before the opener. John had come to the same conclusion I had come to earlier. "After measuring tracks and droppings, it looks like I've got three bucks to hunt, Dad, the Moose Mountain dominant buck, probably a big ten-pointer, a 2-1/2 year-old buck, a six or eight-pointer, and a yearling, a spike or forkie. And I found at least thirty good spots for portable stump hunting."

Following a gala opening day dinner, featuring buck liver and heart smothered in onions, I pointed to our hunting map spread on the table and said to my sons Dave and John, "Tomorrow morning, let's hunt the Moose Mountain dominant buck together. It won't exactly be cover-all-bases buck hunting (see Chapter II). We'll be hunting the same buck, but we won't be keying on buck range elements. We'll be keying on feeding areas of does in three separate doe ranges within the buck's breeding range. Breeding is in progress, or soon will be. Whether that buck searching for a doe in estrus or with a doe in estrus, when the sun comes up tomorrow, the Moose Mountain dominant buck will likely be located where a doe is feeding. Now that our whitetails have turned to browse, the three does I have in mind will be feeding on osier's growing around the perimeter of this big, high basin spruce bog. If we position ourselves on three sides of this bog, one of us is likely to get a crack at that buck.

"John, you know the south and east sides of this bog better than anyone, it being your hunting area, so you get the long, difficult route in the morning. It'll be risky, too. The wind will be from the south, meaning, you'll have to go in somewhat downwind. Ordinarily, that's not the thing to do, but once you are in position, feeding deer will not be able to smell you. To minimize the likelihood of being smelled as you approach the area, head in from the southwest, angling toward the western end of this feeding area, about 100 yards west of that twelve-foot-diameter boulder. When you come to the bog, circle a bit toward the east before sitting down. That way, your scent-laden tracks won't be in front of where you are sitting. Sit low among the thick spruces of the bog, facing the wind and the slope where the deer will be feeding."

"It should be perfect, Dad," John said excitedly. "While scouting briefly in that area, midday, I found lots of fresh tracks and droppings, and a perfect stand site right about where you suggested I should sit. I didn't spot any signs made by the big buck, but the 2-1/2 year-old was definitely there this morning."

"This could mean the big one is with a doe in estrus," I said thoughtfully, "no longer patrolling its breeding range or renewing the buck-repelling musk scents of its ground scrapes and antler rubs. If this is the case, I hope that buck is with one of the does we'll be watching in the morning.

"Dave, you and I will have it easier. We'll circle west of the feeding areas we'll hunt and approach them from downwind. I'll take you to the best spot on the southwest corner of the bog and then I'll circle around to north side."

John's carbine popped twice at 7:20AM. Immediately thereafter, everyone in the gang thought of the same old hunting adage: *one shot, deer; two shots, maybe; three shots, not likely.* At 10:30AM I met John, Peggy, Kevin, Dave and Ken on the trail 200 yards north of camp.

"Well?" I asked.

"I was at a perfect spot," John said. "I had four deer feeding right in front of me, two of them bucks—the yearling and the 2-1/2 year-old. I wounded a buck, Dad." John then added, a worried look on his face. "I think I hit it too far back. I found stomach contents on its trail. I tracked it to the creek valley north of my old tree stand. At that point I decided to quit, giving the deer a chance to lie down, and maybe die, not forcing it to travel a great distance from where it was hit."

"So far, so good," I said. "The rest of you go back to camp. John and I will track this deer alone. This buck is likely to travel all day if pushed by a big, noisy gang. Two hunters working silently will have a much better chance. If we need your help, we'll fire three well-spaced shots."

Upon arriving at the site where the buck was hit, John led me along its trail, explaining what happened. "I was sitting over there," he whispered. "About 7:00AM, the four deer, two of them bucks, walked across that slope from the east. They were moving slowly, feeding among those thick hazels. I had no open shot until the smaller of the two bucks stepped into this opening (30 yards from his stand). When I shot, the buck raced past me into the bog. Figuring it was done for, I turned my attention to the other buck. All I could see was bobbing tails, however, and within the blink of an eye they were gone, disappearing southeast. Then the buck I shot at came out of the bog and stopped under that big pine tree (50 yards away). I shot at it again. It then bounded away toward the northeast.

"I thought I had a perfect heart shot both times. As you can see, however, there is no hair or blood here where the buck stood when I took my first shot. My first bullet hit this one-inch tree branch. In the excitement I didn't notice it. I don't know if my bullet fragmented, ricochetted or passed through this branch intact, but I know I hit the deer. I found a few drops of blood on the trail where it bounded into the bog. After my second shot, it bled more heavily, not spraying small droplets of bright blood to one or both sides like a lung-shot deer, however. From this point on all I found were occasional drops and small pools of dark blood and small, dark-brown gobs of chewed-up browse, all upon or between its tracks. Between here and where I left the trail at the creek valley 200 yards north, the buck did not lie down and the spots of blood seemed to be becoming less common. Do you think we have a chance to recover this buck?"

"Blood is scant and there doesn't seem to be any blood on branches and foliage brushed by the deer's flanks," I answered, kneeling on the buck's trail. "It bounded strongly, tracks well apart (15 feet or more), forming typical elongated C or J patterns. All four legs are functional, hoof-tips together. Normally, when hit in the abdomen, a whitetail's bounds will be short, its body hunched and its tracks bunched, forming squares, diamonds or trapezoids. When you add the fact that the buck did not lie down within 200 yards, it appears this deer was not injured seriously enough to cause a quick death. I think your first bullet caused little damage, perhaps merely a scratch. Your second bullet obviously passed into or through the buck's stomach, I'd guess, very low, doing no damage to major blood vessels. Though unlikely to bleed to death, because of the abdominal wound, this deer will eventually die, but not today, and maybe not even tomorrow, unless we succeed in getting close enough for a finishing shot. We might have a long, tough trail ahead of us. I hope not," I added, looking up at the leaden sky. "It looks like snow."

"You know the routine, John: I'll slowly follow the buck's trail, intent on deer signs, while you keep well to one side, scanning ahead and to either side, ready to fire. We'll move as silently as possible, never conversing with more than a whisper. Be especially alert upon approaching thick cover. That's where a wounded deer will usually lie down and watch its backtrail. I'll whistle softly if I need your help. In this snow trailing shouldn't be too difficult, but as you know, wolf-country buck's know plenty of ways to fool a trailing hunter. This buck will be in full possession of its cunning. It'll be like trailing an unwounded buck, only worse, because this buck will be expecting us, ready to lead us a merry chase."

Whenever a whitetail finds it necessary to raise its tail and flee, it expects pursuit. It will soon halt in dense trailside cover to determine if pursuit is in progress, identifying the pursuer, and the pursuer's speed and location, via sight, sounds and/or airborne scents. Once a safe distance has been gained (100-200 yards in forest cover), it will do many things to ensure its safety and discourage pursuit. It will cling to dense cover to avoid being sighted. It will slow down and begin exercising great stealth to avoid being heard. It will swing into the wind, using its nose to avoid ambushes. It will take to trails of other deer, where it will be difficult to distinguish its tracks (and scent) from tracks of other deer, often changing direction and sometimes reversing direction. It will push through or leap over obstacles and make use of terrain (swampy or steep) that discourage pursuit. It will rest at sites where it can spot a pursuer on its backtrail at a safe distance. It will make use of noisy cover or terrain where it will be easy to pinpoint via hearing the location of a pursuer at a safe distance. It can endlessly outmaneuver an unseen pursuer in dense cover, maintaining a safe distance by keeping track of the pursuer's movements via airborne scent and/or sounds alone.

Despite good tracking snow, within minutes after John and I split up at the creek valley I lost the buck's trail. The deer had slowed to a walk and the valley was loaded with fresh deer tracks of a similar size. Blood or stomach contents from the wounded deer were now reduced to one or two small dark spots half buried in the soft snow every 5-20 yards and they were practically indistinguishable from spots of wet soil dropped from hoofs of other deer unless picked up and flattened between the fingers. By walking ever-larger half-circles in the direction taken by the deer from the last blood sign, the direction indicated by squares of toilet paper spindled on tips of overhanging branches along the buck's trail, we eventually picked up its trail again. At this point, the wounded buck's tracks mingled with those of two other deer heading north. Near the top of the north side of the valley, the wounded deer turned east toward a hazel smothered knob overlooking the valley—a typical spot where a wounded buck is likely to bed. I whistled, catching John's attention, and pointed vigorously toward the promontory.

As I pushed through the hazels to the top, I discovered I had guessed right, but much too late. The buck had bedded there, all right, but it was gone. Pools of blood mixed with stomach contents in its bed outlined by the snow indicated John's bullet had passed through the deer exactly where I had surmised. The position of the pools in the bed and the fact that the entry and exit wounds were only about eight inches apart substantiated a very low paunch hit. Upon abandoning its bed, the buck headed east, downhill, paralleling the gurgling creek that rushed from the spruce bog behind us to the deep river valley far below. The deer had not bounded, indicating it had spotted us and departed while we were yet a safe distance away. Though we had not yet spotted the buck, at this point I figured we were little more than 100 yards from our quarry. However, after having bedded for about four hours, bleeding had stopped, clotting complete and/or the deer having thoroughly licked its wounds.

"If this buck's tracks become mingled with fresh tracks of other deer again," I whispered to John, "we'll be in big trouble. And look at that—it's starting to snow."

A quarter-mile east, our quarry turned south, back into the creek valley, and then headed west, following the stream. Within a clump of alders about 200 yards upstream, we discovered a spot where it had stood frozen, obviously watching us as we passed higher up, following its trail toward the east. As I had feared, the buck's tracks soon led across our tracks where we had originally crossed the stream and disappeared into the maze of tracks that stymied us earlier. Having no idea where the buck went from there, John and I began tracing ever-widening spirals about the the last square of toilet tissue marking its trail. About thirty minutes later, on a well-tracked deer trail near the crest of the south side of the valley, I whistled. As John approached, I pointed toward blood, lots of blood.

"Its wounds have started bleeding again," I whispered, "probably due to the exertions of climbing these steep slopes. From this point on, we'll stick doggedly to its trail, moving a little faster so those wounds won't have a chance to clot shut again. If the buck loses enough blood, it may weaken enough to allow us to get closer."

About fifty yards up the trail I came to a halt, muttering, "Now what!" The copious bleeding had suddenly ended. "How could that happen?" I pondered.

After carefully inspecting the trail ahead, it became obvious the buck

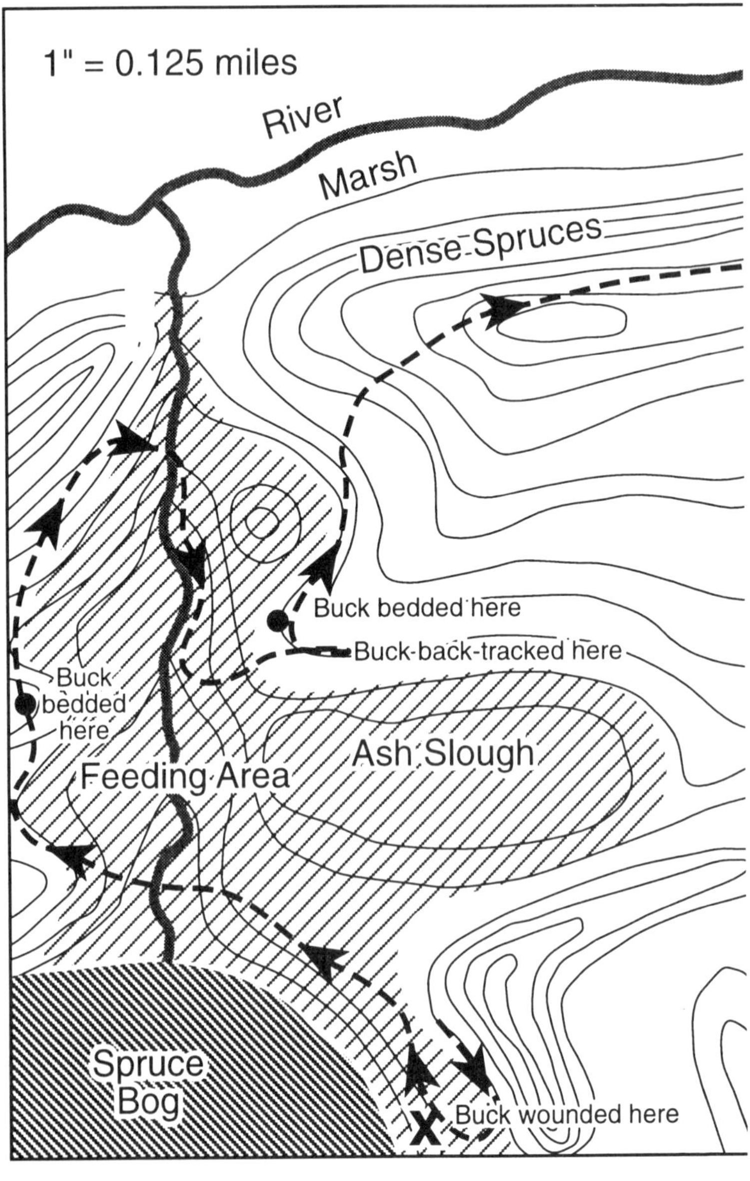
1" = 0.125 miles
River
Marsh
Dense Spruces
Buck bedded here
Buck back-tracked here
Buck bedded here
Ash Slough
Feeding Area
Spruce Bog
Buck wounded here

117

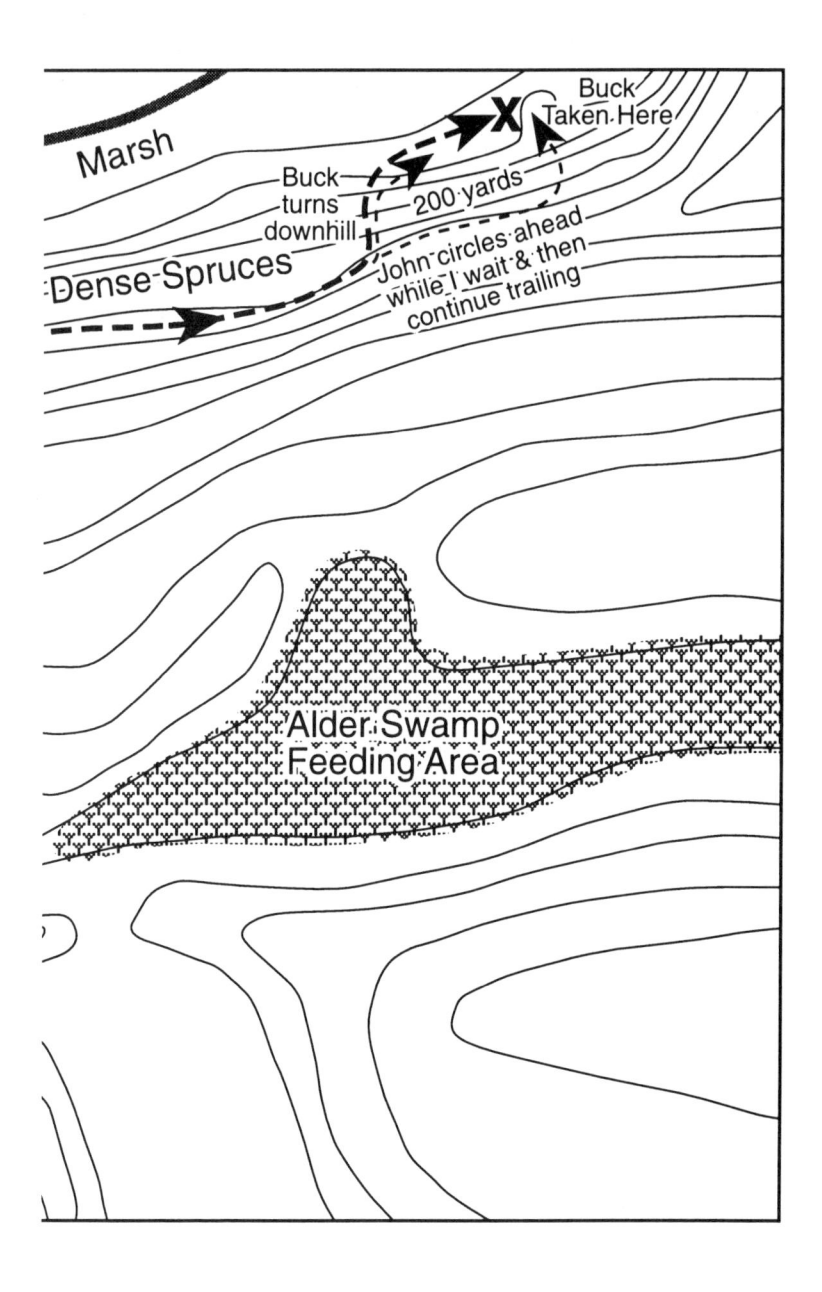

Marsh

Buck Taken Here

X

Buck turns downhill

200 yards

Dense Spruces

John circles ahead while I wait & then continue trailing

Alder Swamp Feeding Area

had left the trail, but where? While standing next to a large balsam tree ten yards back from where the blood trail ended, deer tracks beneath the tree's boughs, hanging a mere foot from the ground, caught my eye—attention. Dropping to hands and knees, I crawled through the base of the tree, following the tracks. On the opposite side of the tree I found myself staring into another bloody deer bed. Inches from my face, I could see blood spreading outward in the snow. "John," I sharply whispered, "it's close; very close. Get over here quick and look around!"

"Nope," John whispered shortly, "I don't see it."

While following the bloody trail of the buck through the dense evergreens and windfalls nearly one-half mile south of its last bed, I again halted and whistled to John. At this point, we were near the top of a steep and treacherous, heavily-wooded slope that paralleled the wide, grassy river bed several hundred yards below.

"Look here, John," I whispered, "I think we're getting close to the end of this trail. The buck's toes are now widely spread, not together as before. The buck is also dragging its hoofs over logs, not stepping or leaping over them cleanly like before. It's obviously weakening, likely because of blood loss. It's also beginning to zigzag like a deer heading into a bedding area. I think this buck is anxious to lie down, but it probably doesn't dare because we are too near."

"It's amazing," John said, shaking his head, scanning ahead. "We've been very close to this buck for a good two hours, but we haven't seen it even once."

"Soon, John, soon," I said.

Fifty yards ahead, I again halted, whistling softly and beckoning vigorously.

"The buck turned and headed straight downhill," I whispered excitedly. "Going down this steep slope is the only way it could gain some distance on us and get it a chance to rest. See that thick line of evergreens along the edge of the open river valley? That's the only place the buck could be right now. Head south about 200 yards or so, staying at this level on the mountain. That's about all the distance you'll need to travel to get ahead of the buck. Then move silently down to that line of evergreens and wait. In fifteen minutes I'll start after the buck again, pushing it toward you. This should do it. Good luck."

Half-way down the steep, treacherous slope, grabbing tree branches and saplings to keep from sliding, I noticed the buck's tracks were veering left. "Darn," I silently moaned, "I hope he didn't turn back toward the north." A short distance lower, the tracks veered right, and from my vantage point I could see the buck's tracks leading south in the desired direction. Before

I could take another step, the river valley reverberated with the sound of a gunshot, followed almost immediately by the shouted words, "Got 'im!"

Following traditional congratulations and handshakes, photography and field dressing, John and I sat down to rest, girding ourselves for the exhausting 1-1/2 mile drag over the mountain yet before us and reflecting on what we had accomplished.

A successful conclusion: a rightfully proud son, and behind the camera, an equally proud father.

"Dad," John finally said, "I am very thankful you were here to help me today. The way you figured out what to do, especially during the last hour, was uncanny. I could not have done it myself. For that matter, I don't think anyone else could have done it. Without your help, I would have never recovered this deer. I'm especially thankful to be free of the thought that there is a deer out here, doomed, suffering and wasted because of I had done. It was tough, but we did it. We fulfilled our hunter's obligation."

"During the coming years," I responded, "I'm sure we will again find ourselves obligated to undertake the same task. Sometimes it can't be helped. Deer sometimes move a split second before the trigger is pulled, and unseen branches sometimes deflect bullets or arrows. Nonetheless, as well as it ended today, I truly wish it would never happen again. Especially when hunting whitetails, an ounce of prevention *is* worth a pound of cure. Before this day is done, we'll feel as if we spent a thousand pounds for the cure. What I'm getting at is this: it's time to retire your carbine. Next season, I don't care what it takes, I want you to carry a drop-em-in-their-tracks rifle like mine."

"I agree," John answered. "I've been plagued by the same thought all day. I wanted to buy a 7mm Magnum this year, but it just didn't work out. What happened today was the last straw. Rest assured, this is the last time I will use this carbine to hunt whitetails."

"That's great, John," I said with a smile. "Well, let's get your buck up that mountain."

Another exceptionally elusive buck that fell victim to three hunters (from left to right, Ken Nordberg, the author and Kevin Stone) using the "cover-all-bases" approach. Sometimes it's not enough to know where a buck feeds, beds and travels. Older bucks rarely use the same trail twice in a row and travel off-trail at least 50% of the time. Putting three skilled Johnny-on-the-spot buck hunters in the hunt increases the odds for success by three, often with startlingly quick results.

Chapter 3

Cover-All-Bases Buck Hunting

Like in Johnny-on-the-spot buck hunting, the wolves of northern Minnesota played a role in the development of the small-group hunting method I refer to as "cover-all-bases buck hunting." In this case, however, the hunting methods of wolves did not provide the impetus. It was desperation, being occasionally forced to enlist the aid of my sons, daughters and son-in-law to take adult bucks made extra wary by the year-around hunting of over-abundant gray wolves.

Definition

"Cover-all-bases buck hunting" is three or four Johnny-on-the-spot buck hunters hunting the same adult buck, all using pre-selected stand sites within 10–50 yards of widely separated trails or sites currently frequented by the quarry.

Personal experience has taught me two hunters are not enough for this hunting method, success not materially improved, and five or more are too many, the quarry commonly alarmed before the hunters can reach their pre-selected stand sites.

Though the "cover-all-bases" approach has thus far been successful in two of every three attempts at taking adult bucks (when used by the Nordberg hunting gang), I generally consider it a "last ditch" hunting method, one I'll only use when hunting time is running short and/or when a certain buck has proven to be especially difficult to ambush via Johnny-on-the-spot buck hunting. I have four reasons. First, I much prefer hunting adult bucks one-on-one. Second, the cover-all-bases method is a somewhat aggressive form of hunting, the risk of alarming an intended quarry considerably greater than when hunting a buck one-on-one. If not taken, alarm sufficient enough to lead to range abandonment generally occurs within 1–2 half-days of cover-all-bases buck hunting. Third, this method cannot be used until stand sites within 10–50 yards of trails or sites currently frequented by the quarry are located for each hunter. This generally takes two or more days of mid-hunt scouting and three or more half-days of hunting. Fourth, though highly effective, you never know which of the hunters will shoot the buck. All have an equal chance.

It should also be noted, cover-all-bases buck hunting is definitely not for everyone. I don't believe *all* hunters can use it with equal success. Each hunter taking part must be a very skilled whitetail hunter, or better, a very skilled Johnny-on-the-spot buck hunter. One bad apple in the bunch, one who lacks adequate stealth or patience or insists on doing things differently, will invariably ruin the hunt for everyone. I personally would never include a hunter I could not trust to avoid talking out loud, find a preselected stand site or remain seated at a designated spot until the quarry is taken or it is 11AM or sunset.

The heaviest and one of the most elusive bucks we Nordbergs have ever taken fell victim to cover-all-bases buck last November. The following tale of this hunt, "Antler Mountain Showdown," provides an excellent means of explaining everything that should be known to make this hunting method as effective as it can be.

Chapter 4

Antler Mountain Showdown

The Gentle Nudge, Johnny-on-the-Spot and Cover-All-Bases Buck Hunting

"Where are you going to start, Dad?" Ken asked as he poked a couple chunks of split popple into the crackling maw of the barrel stove.

"As usual, I'm prepared to hunt three adult bucks," I answered, "but the Moose Mountain dominant buck, the one that made those rubs on six to eight-inch pines near the feeding area where Katy got her ten-pointer last year, has me most interested right now. I think I'll start right here," I said, pointing to an X on our hunting map. "While scouting at noon today, I found this buck's fresh tracks fifty yards from this stand site. The buck approached the feeding area from the east, followed a trail around the north end of the spruce bog, and then went back the same way. Though such bucks rarely use the same trail twice in a row, having not been hunted yet, I'm hoping it will do the same thing tomorrow morning.

"I wish we had spotted signs of breeding today, bucks dragging their hoofs from track to track (a sign we refer to as railroad tracks). Breeding should be in progress right now. Maybe it has started elsewhere, but we saw no evidence of it in the areas in which we did our last-minute scouting today. If we had found evidences of breeding, we'd be planning a gentle nudge or two right now, like last year (a new hunting method introduced in *Whitetail Hunter's Almanac, 6th Edition*).

"What about you?" I asked.

"I'm heading straight west across the swamp to that second ridge overlooking that feeding area next to the beaver pond," Ken said. "The wind will be perfect for that spot in the morning. While checking that ridge at noon today, I didn't see any tracks or droppings of the big buck that regularly fed there last fall. Wolves probably got it last winter, being as old as it was. I did find tracks of a younger buck, however. They were only five-inchers, meaning the buck is a 2-1/2 year-old. Considering we put that mineral block near that buck bedding area 200 yards north of there last spring, it should have fairly decent antlers."

"Well," I said, glancing at the clock, "it's time to put the stew on the stove. The rest of our gang will begin showing up at any time."

Day One

"What a strange opening morning," Peggy said, sliding a hot platter of eggs onto the table. "Not a shot fired."

"Strange for us, anyway," Dave added. "We usually have at least one buck hanging in camp by now."

"We'll have one this evening," Ken said, grinning. "Dad, that buck I'm hunting is with a doe in estrus. On the way in I ran across its railroad tracks, along with the tracks of a doe and fawn, near the south end of that feeding area. The deer were heading toward the doe's bedding area in that low grassy area northwest of the next beaver pond south. You know that area better than anyone. After lunch, how about being my upwind man on a gentle nudge?"

"I'd have to circle at least a mile and a half," I mused, "but I suppose we ought do it. Our gentle nudge has never failed under these circumstances. Where will you be?"

"On that knob at the south end of that ridge," Ken said.

An hour and fifteen minutes after leaving camp, I found myself standing on a small rise overlooking the southwestern edge of the doe bedding area. Nothing stirred. Off to my left, the seed-laden tips of the grasses of a flooded marsh bent in the breeze from left to right. To make certain my scent would spread throughout the entire bedding area, I decided to move west another 100 yards before sitting down. I could see it would be a tough 100 yards, thick with alders, windfalls and muddy pools of water. but I had to stick close to the edge of the marsh to make certain I would not end up between Ken and the deer.

While slipping beneath some interlacing alders about half-way to my destination, a twig snapped a short distance ahead. I rose quickly and glimpsed three deer racing northeast, straight toward Ken. Shortly, two deer veered southeast, logically the doe and fawn. I looked at my watch. Five seconds passed...ten seconds...twenty...*Kaboom!*

It was the familiar, thunderous roar of **Ken's 7mm Magnum.**

Following a brisk hike toward the site of the shot, I halted and said out loud, "Where are you?"

"Over here," Ken answered, surprisingly near. I couldn't see him because of the thickness of the hazels and alders between us.

"Where's the buck?" I asked.

Ken had this 2-1/2 year-old buck figured to a "T."

"About ten yards in front of you," he answered. "When I shot, it dropped in its tracks. That sure didn't take long. It's only 2:30."

"Nice buck," I presently said, "a big 2-1/2 year-old with a nice eight-point rack, just like you figured. While we're dressing it out, I'll tell you all about why you got it so quickly."

Day Two

In the pre-dawn darkness on Sunday morning I placed my portable stool on frozen muskeg and sat down behind the upturned roots of a windfallen spruce 100 yards south of my opening morning stand site. Thirty yards before me was the junction of two deer trails: one the perimeter trail of the feeding area; the other a trail that led toward my quarry's mountaintop bedding area. Tracks made by that buck during the previous 2–24 hours were on both trails. An hour after first light, I heard a deer pass from right to left, but I could not see it (tracks discovered later revealed it was my intended quarry).

At 10:20AM two muffled shots echoed about a half mile due east----the area John was hunting (John's story, "On the Trail of a Wounded Buck," is featured in Chapter 2).

Day Three

"Shoot," I grunted while pulling on my boots early the next morning.

"What?" Dave asked, lacing his.

"It just occurred to me that feeding area I've been hunting might be ruined. John and I had to drag his buck through a good portion of it after sunset yesterday, right about the time that buck would have been feeding there."

My concern was well-founded. Not only was the feeding area completely devoid of deer and fresh signs Monday morning, but

A disheartening discovery---the big buck bounded into the bog.

1" = 0.125 miles

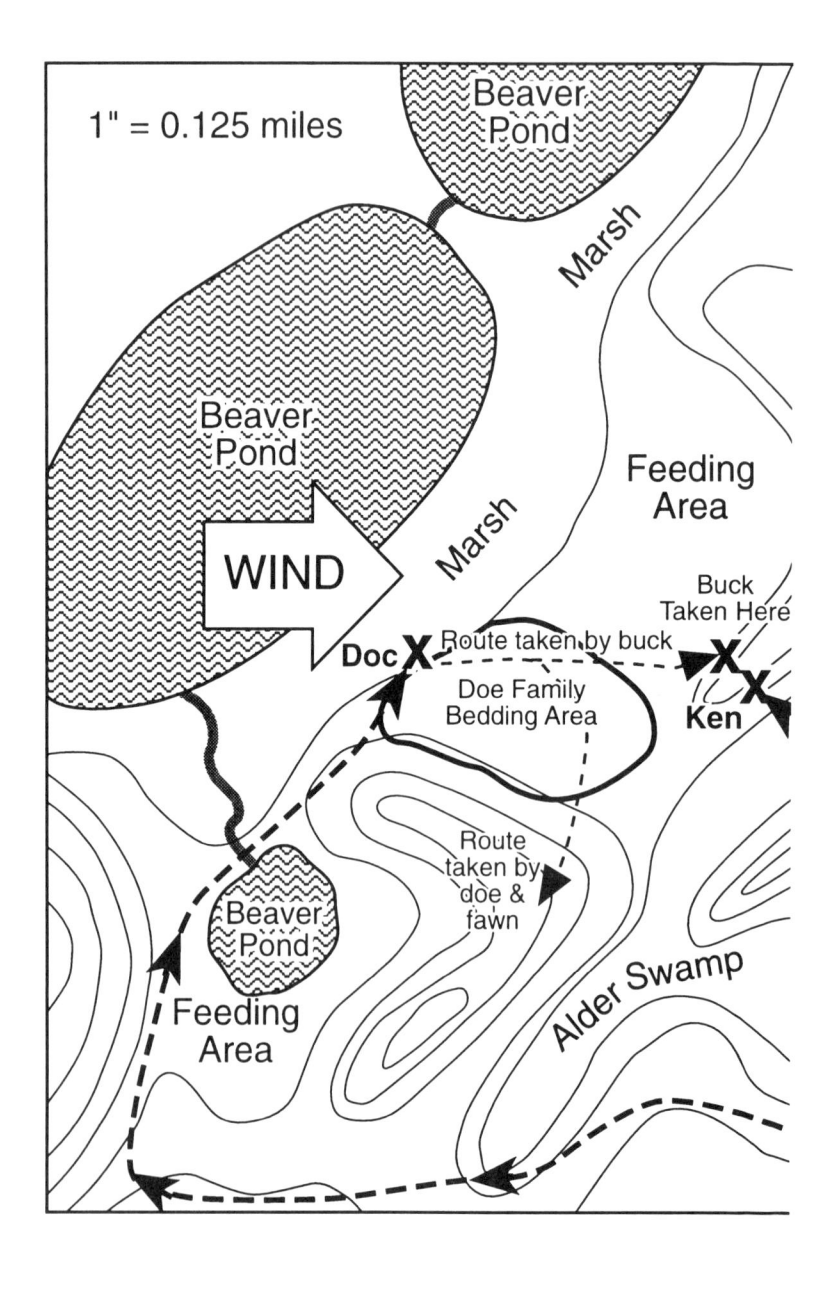

127

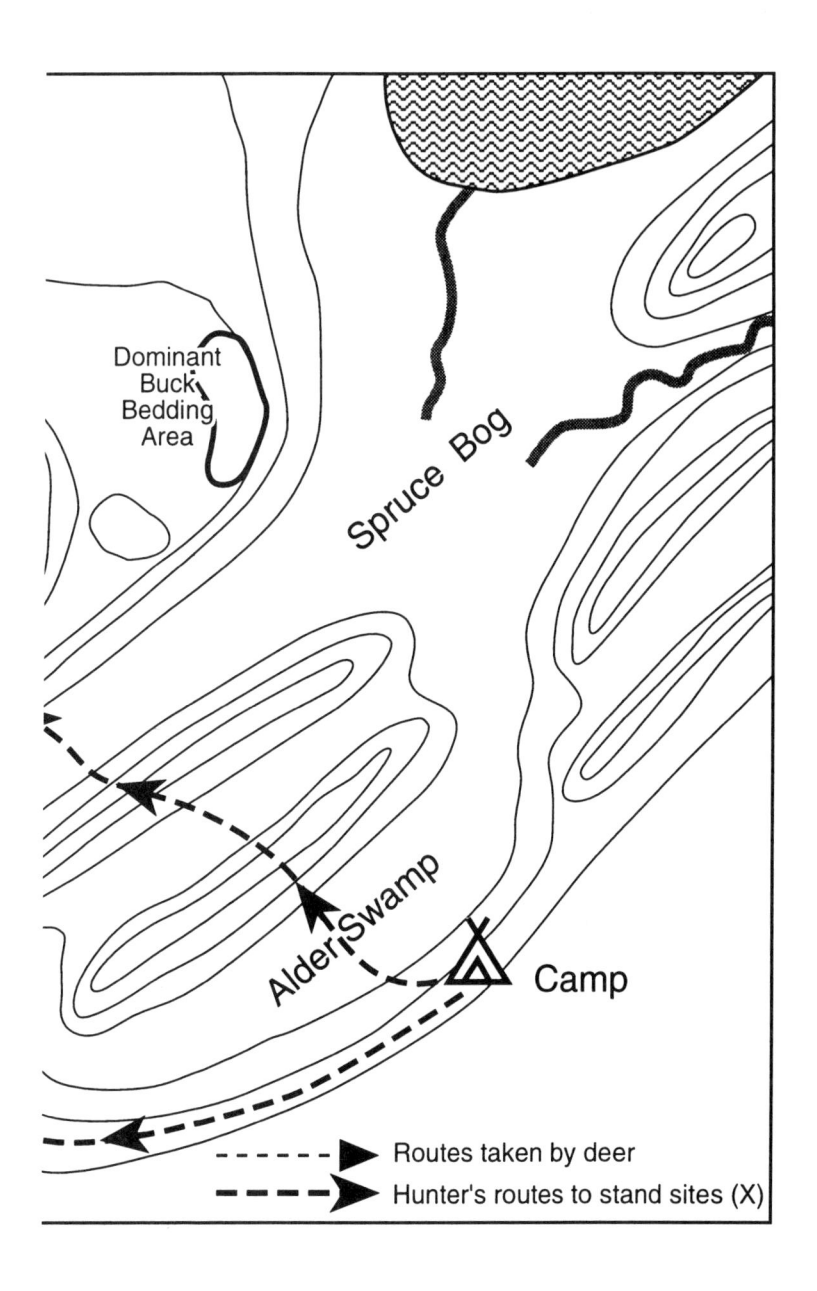

while scouting midday 200 yards southeast of where I sat, I discovered bad news—elongated J-patterns of the buck I hunted, a good 25 feet apart. Tracks in the snow indicated the buck had been feeding on osier browse at the very time John and I were struggling westward. Upon hearing or spotting us approaching, it bounded headlong into the spruce bog. This meant, of course, the hunt for this buck was over for a period of 5-10 days, maybe longer. It was time to turn to buck number-two.

At noon, after Peggy, Kevin, John and Ken loaded up and began their long trek home, Dave and I sat down for coffee and a round of cribbage.

"I hate to think of it, but I have to head home tomorrow," Dave said, shuffling the cards. "So far, I haven't seen a deer."

"Come to think of it," I reflected, "I've only had glimpses of three, and now I have to start all over again.

"I'll tell you what, in about an hour I'm planning to hike to my favorite hunting area two miles north. It has not been hunted yet and the wind is right for entering the area from the creek crossing. If you're interested, why don't you come along. Having not been there in nearly a month, finding stand sites will be strictly guesswork, but we can't go far wrong if we key on known browse areas. I can drop you off at a spot near the north side of one of the better feeding areas, a high-basin loaded with red osier, black ash saplings and mountain maples. I'm planning to sit at the rim of the deep valley on the other side of Birch Mountain, another favorite feeding area."

"Sounds good," Dave said, dealing. "With that quarter-moon riding high, though, the odds for seeing deer this evening won't be too favorable. Your cut. When there is moonlight in the evening, these darn wolf-country whitetails almost always wait until sunset to begin feeding."

"True," I said, "but you never know. We've taken two in the evening during the past three seasons. Favorable or not, I'm anxious to get up there and do a little scouting. I need to learning something about the current movements of that dominant buck. Somewhere between the creek and that valley, I should run across signs that will put me close to that buck tomorrow morning."

Tracks in snow indicated a doe and its yearling and fawn were feeding in the high basin browse area daily. I did not find fresh tracks of the dominant buck until I swung south to skirt the open top of Birch Mountain. Still not dragging its hoofs from track to track, the buck had emerged from the southwest corner of the feeding area sometime in the morning. Before turning in the general direction of Antler Mountain, barely visible through the trees a quarter-mile southwest, the buck had stopped to renew a ground scrape. Obviously, no doe in its breeding range was currently in estrus. Typical of phase II of the rut, this buck was still cruising scrape trails and would yet be regularly returning to its previously located bedding area on the northeast end of the high, rocky ridge southeast of Antler Mountain.

A mournful chorus of wolves far to the west ended the day. As I stood up to strap my stool to my back, a branch snapped smartly back in the direction of Antler Mountain.

"You've been staring at that map and shaking your head for thirty minutes," Dave said. "What's up?"

"No matter how I try to figure it," I answered, "I've got a tough trip ahead of me in the morning. I want to be sitting on the northern tip of Antler Mountain at first light, overlooking one of the dominant buck's scrape trails. This particular trail runs the entire length of its oblong breeding range. Wherever that buck is at first light, feeding where it fed this morning or cruising scrape routes, this trail included, it will eventually end up at the north end of Antler Mountain, turning south along one side or the other to get to its bedding area. With the wind expected to be from the northwest in the morning, to get to there without running the risk of being smelled by that buck, I'm going to have begin by skirting the west side of that string of four beaver ponds south of the creek crossing. Then I'll have to make a wide detour around the east side of the buck's bedding area and approach Antler Mountain from the southeast, rounding the northern tip in heavy cover well below the open top. To do all this, I'll have to travel in darkness through two big alder swamps, no marked trails anywhere along the entire route. This means I'll need to start at least an hour early tomorrow."

"Don't wake me 'til you're ready to leave," Dave said.

Day Four

A red squirrel softly chirred its "good morning" as the blackness of the sighing balsams below began to take on a greenish hue. Scattered beneath the balsams, 40–70 yards upwind, the adult doe of the area and her yearling doe and fawn traded sentinel duties as they eagerly cropped succulent tips of of red osiers. Moving slowly west, they disappeared from sight as the first rays of the sun began breaking through the trees behind me. I leaned back against the trunk of an ancient Norway pine, finally relaxing. Almost immediately, a motion caught my eye on my left. As I slowly turned my head, a monstrous buck, its neck grotesquely enlarged, stepped silently through a narrow opening beneath a particularly dense clump of balsams some fifty yards away. My heart pounding, I eased the safety of my rifle forward and waited with baited breath. But nothing happened. Rather than continue north past my stand site, the unseen buck turned northwest, likely drawn by the airborne scents of the three female deer that passed a short time earlier.

At 11AM I threw in the towel and began some cautious scouting. After inspecting the six-inch-long tracks of the buck below, I headed south along the western rim of Antler Mountain, intending to cross to the opposite side via a brushy saddle. There, however, I came to an abrupt halt 20 yards short a much-used deer trail. From my vantage point, I could see it was loaded with fresh and old tracks of the dominant buck. This was obviously a favorite route to its bedding area located about 200 yards due east. Deciding this would be my next stand site, rather than cross this trail (fearful of tainting it with ruinous human trail scent which persists 24–48 hours), I reversed direction and headed back to camp via the Birch Mountain trail I used the previous evening. Half-way around the north side of the high-basin feeding area, I again came upon hours-old tracks of the big buck. After leaving the does, it had apparently traveled north to the deep river valley on my left, swung back through the feeding area it had visited the day before and returned to its bedding area via the east side of Antler Mountain (it obviously did not return via the west side where I spent the morning).

The trail across the Antler Mountain saddle—a favorite of my 8-point quarry.

Dave was just finishing loading hunting gear into his car as I topped the ridge just north of camp an hour later.

"No dice?" he presently asked.

"No dice," I answered, nonetheless grinning. "He's big, really big. I saw four deer this morning, including the dominant buck. It's just a matter of time before I get him, I think. I've now got him pretty well figured out."

"We've all said that before," Dave reminded me. "If you get him, rather than drag it to camp yourself like the last time you took a big buck in that area, winch him high in a tree until some of the others return this weekend. I won't be back until next Monday or Tuesday. Good luck," he added as he drove away.

Day Five

"One...two...three..." I counted silently, watching and listening intently. "Where's the buck?"

It was 7:05 AM. An adult doe, yearling doe and fawn had just crossed a moss-covered slab of granite about 70 yards southwest of where I sat and they were now devouring osier tips in a small hazel-covered opening just to the left. They had no idea I was near. I was sitting crosswind, leaning back against a sappy trunk in the center of a tepee-like enclosure formed by the sagging boughs of a big balsam tree.

The decision to hunt at this spot came the moment I leaped across a small, gurgling creek 100 yards east an hour or so earlier. As I landed, my flashlight beam came to rest on very fresh, six-inch-long deer tracks. Obviously, my quarry had been drinking at this spot hours, perhaps minutes, earlier. From there, the buck walked (obviously unalarmed) up the trail I had planned to use to get to the east side of Antler Mountain. At the top of the slope overlooking the creek, the buck turned from the trail and headed south toward the eastern tip of the high basin feeding area. Reasoning the buck was feeding in this area at this very moment, and might return to the creek to drink before heading to its bedding area, I cut to my left, moved south about 50 yards and settled in for a 5–6 hour sit beneath this inviting balsam, about 25 yards downwind of the buck's fresh tracks. But the buck didn't show up.

At noon I headed toward Antler Mountain, scouting into the wind along the north and and then the west side of the feeding area as I went. What I mumbled to myself when I got to the site I originally intended to hunt that morning is unprintable. Fresh tracks indicated the buck had passed within 40 yards an hour or two earlier, heading up the sloping valley on the east side of Antler Mountain toward its bedding area, about 300 yards SSW.

Near the south end of Antler Mountain lies the low, brushy saddle through which this buck often travels to or from its bedding area. Found weeks earlier near the crest of the bald-top mountain, on its east side, stands a lone, six-foot pine tree, thick and nearly as wide as it is tall. Because it overlooks the saddle and the route most recently used by this buck, I decided this tree would make a perfect stand site for the rest of the day.

As it turned out, it wasn't a bad choice. The trouble was, as the buck moved west through the saddle an hour before dark, it kept to the south side. Hidden by thick, intervening brush the whole way. I only saw it once, quite unexpectedly, too briefly to even consider a shot.

Day Six

As the sky began to brighten on the eastern horizon, a pine marten making its morning rounds suddenly halted ten feet from my newest stand site forty yards southwest of the Antler Mountain saddle. The marten rose up on its haunches and starred at me a long minute, its nose wiggling from side to side. It seemed confused by my strange scent. In this deep wilderness area, it is likely I was the first human it had ever smelled. Some minutes after it departed, unafraid, it occurred to me something was wrong. That marten should not have smelled me. It was supposed to be upwind. I wetted a finger and raised it above my head. "Oh no," I silently moaned, "the breeze has switched direction." My scent was now not only blowing toward the saddle, but toward the buck's bedding area 150 yards east.

After looping south and then east and finally north through the densely timbered valley that separates Antler Mountain from the craggy ridge where the buck's bedding area is located, I sat down among a tangle of windfalls, 50 yards crosswind of a trail that was used by the buck the evening before (revealed by fresh tracks leading toward the bedding area). An hour later, I silently moaned again. The capricious wind had switched another 90-degrees. Fearful of ruining the the security of the buck's bedding area, I decided to abandon the area altogether.

Detouring widely, I cautiously made my way back to the east end of the high basin feeding area. Much to my dismay, I discovered tracks indicating the buck had spent a great deal of time feeding in the opening where I had watched the doe, yearling and fawn feeding the morning before. "At this very moment," I then realized, looking at my watch, "it is probably walking past the site I just left." Taking to my previously used Birch Mountain trail, I headed west again. Beneath another drooping balsam beneath drooping balsam 150 yards southeast of the northern end of Antler Mountain, I sat down to eat my lunch. Fifty yards before me was the trail used by the buck as it headed back to its bedding area that morning, likely passing the site while I was scratching my head at the east end of the feeding area less than two hours earlier. "This is becoming ridiculous," I chided myself.

A strong wind and stinging salt-like pellets of snow ended the day's hunt at 3PM.

Day Seven

It was blowing and snowing heavily as I zipped up the tent an hour and a half before sunrise on Friday morning. According to the latest weather forecast, the snow would let up about noon, but the wind would remain strong from the northwest, gusting up to 30 mph, throughout the day. Though the buck would probably remain in its bedding area throughout the day, I decided to hunt anyway, and headed north along the ridge on the west side of the beaver ponds to the downwind perimeter of a favorite browse area directly south of the buck's bedding area. As expected, nothing stirred all day.

At 11PM I awoke to the sounds of car doors slamming out in front of the tent. As I lit the lantern, Ken and Kevin burst through the door flap.

"What are you doing here?" I asked Ken, sitting up and stretching, "and where's Peggy?" I asked Kevin.

"After what Dave told me Tuesday night, I figured you'd need help dragging in that big buck," Ken answered.

"Peggy couldn't find a sitter," Kevin added.

"Well, how big is it?" Ken asked with a grin.

"Real big, but I don't have it yet," I admitted. "That darn buck has been running me ragged all week. I've been within 50–100 yards or so of it at least eight times, but I've only glimpsed it twice. Since the first morning I saw it, wherever I sat, on one side of Antler Mountain, one side of its bedding area or or one side of its feeding area, it used a trail on the opposite side, usually out of sight. As predictable as it is, that darn buck never uses the same trail twice in a row, and it's just as likely to travel off-trail. It's still there, still visiting the same feeding area sometime between first light and 10AM and still moving up one side or the other of Antler Mountain to get to its bedding area sometime between 10AM and 11AM.

"I had planned to break camp on Sunday, so I'm running out of time. Tomorrow morning, I want you two to give me a hand with this buck. We're going to use our cover-all-bases buck hunting method. I've got three perfect stand sites in mind—one near the buck's feeding area, one on Antler Mountain and one near its bedding area. With three of us at these sites in the morning, one of us is sure to get a crack at that buck."

"To make this work, everything will have to be done exactly right. We don't want to alarm this buck getting to our stand sites. Once we are all safely seated, alerting it is okay, which is all that is likely to happen if the buck gets downwind of any of us. As in the past, a little alerting might even work to our advantage. Unaccustomed to dealing with more than one hunter, while intent upon avoiding any hunter it has identified, it will be more likely to blunder into one of the other two hunters.

"The wind will be from the northwest in the morning, almost perfect for what I have in mind. Ken, you know how to get to Antler Mountain in the dark via Four Bear Hill and the creek crossing. I want you and Kevin to use that route in the morning. Take Kevin to that stand site we selected before the hunting season two years ago, the site on the north side of the high basin feeding area. To get there, turn due south at the big boulder on top of the second ridge past the creek crossing. It's about 75 yards in. The northern edge of that feeding area courses from northwest to southeast. Deer within that feeding area should not be able to smell Kevin at that stand site. Then

134

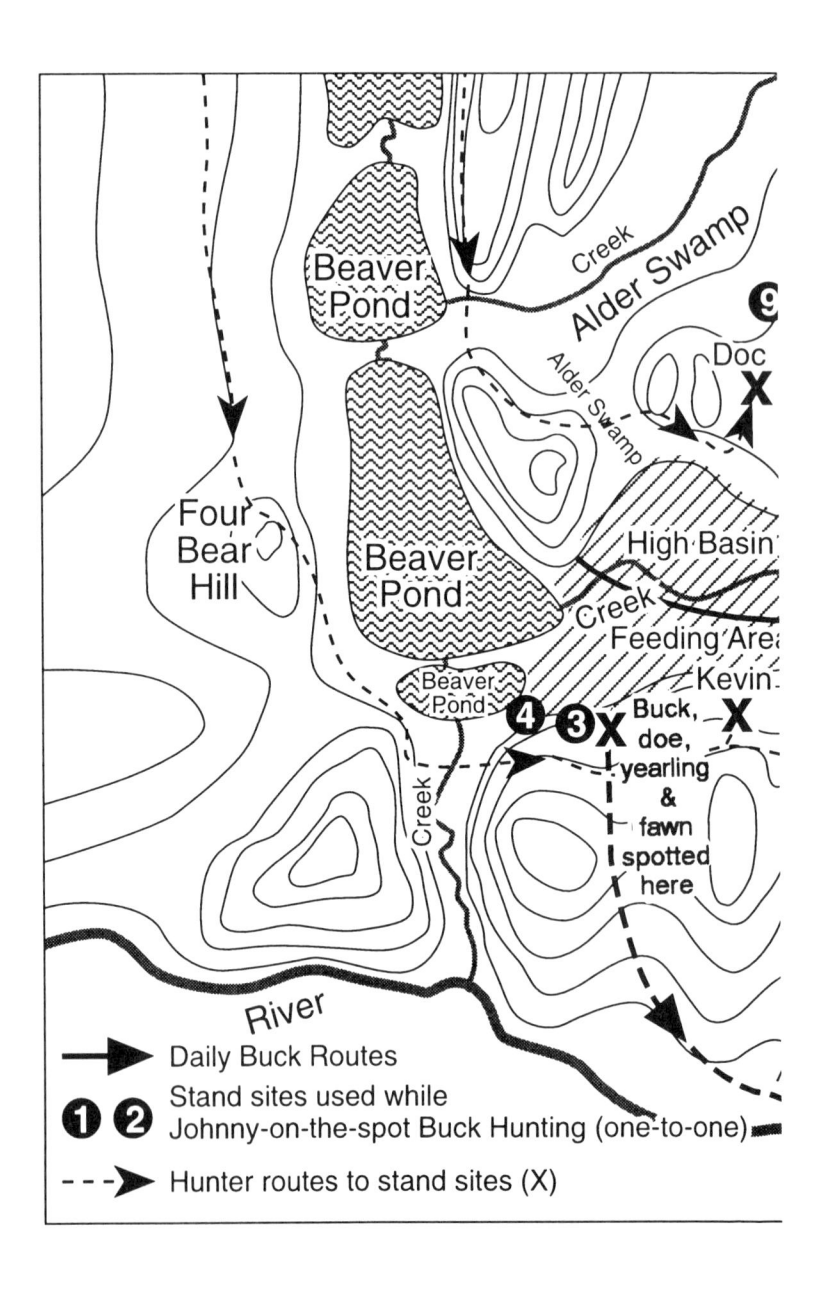

135

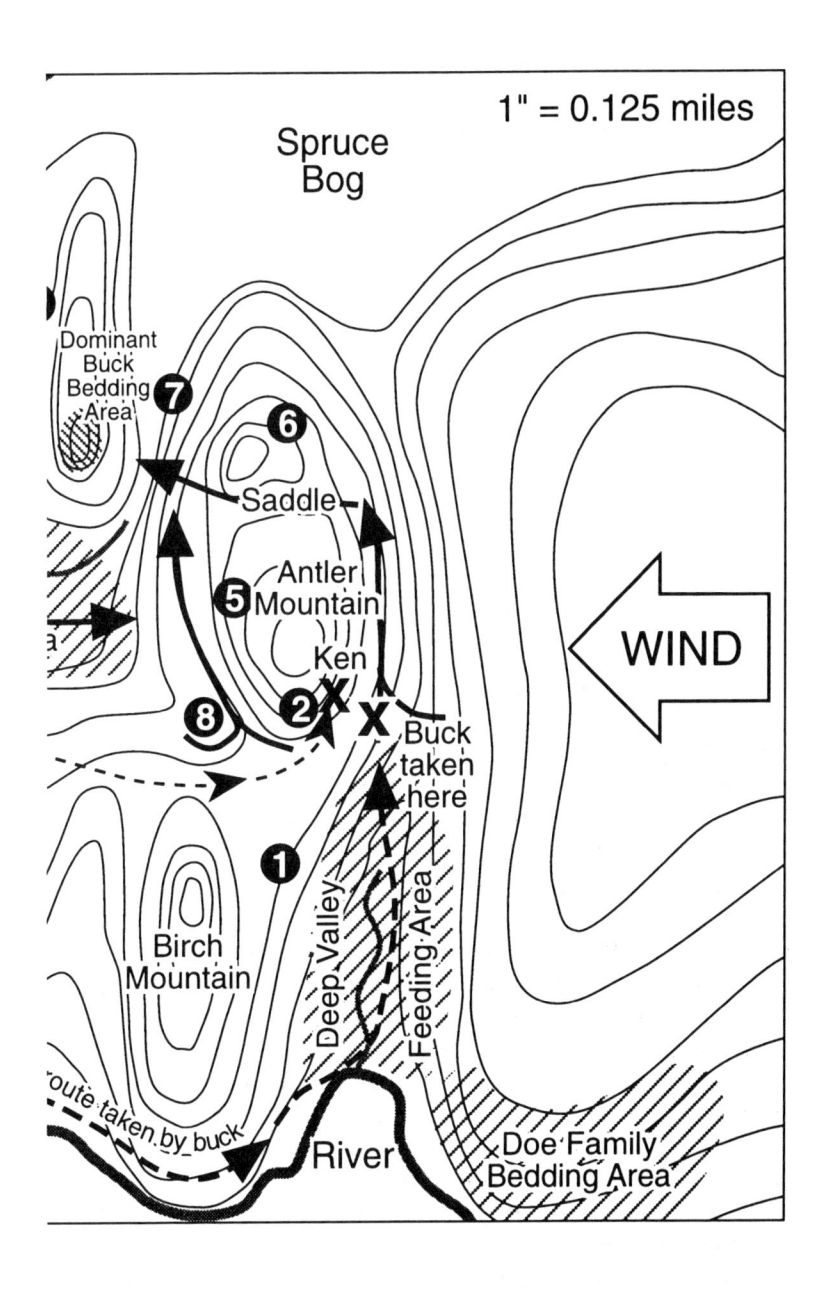

go on past Birch Mountain to that spot on Antler Mountain where you took that seven-pointer two years ago. Meanwhile, I'll head up the west side of the ponds to a spot from which I will be able to keep an eye on the buck's bedding area.

"You guys had better get to bed," I added, looking at the clock. "We're getting up in four hours."

Day Eight

Upon punching in the alarm button the next morning, I jumped to the front of our big wall tent, zipped open the door and peered outside, flashlight in hand. "It's snowing," I groaned.

"Are we going?" a muffled voice inquired.

"I'm not sure," I answered, staring at snowflakes falling through the beam of my flashlight. "It might be snowing hard enough to keep whitetails in their beds, and it might not be. If it isn't and they're moving, this snow will be to our advantage, covering our trail scents and giving us extra cover. I think we should give it a try." I finally said.

My stand site was a clump of stunted oaks next to a granite out-cropping. Within fifteen minutes I was plastered with wet, sticky snow, wishing I had picked a mature evergreen. None being near, I draped plastic bags over my shoulders, thighs, the bore of my rifle and my rifle scope.

At 10AM, a sudden movement caught my eye. Before I could move, a doe walked to the top of the adjacent outcropping. After peering about several long seconds, it looked downward. It obviously didn't like what it saw. Whatever that big, snow-covered lump was down there, it seemed to be alive. This being the case, the doe decided to depart, rapidly, almost kicking snow in my face.

Twenty minutes later I heard a sound akin to a large metal door being slammed shut. According to my compass, the sound came from due north. "Kevin got the buck," I concluded, rising to my feet and brushing off snow.

A swift, downhill hike soon brought me to Kevin's stand. No one was in sight. While I stood there pondering what to do, that large metal door slammed three more times (the traditional Nordberg signal for assistance), due west. "It was *Ken,*" I then realized. Intervening Antler Mountain, the wind and the heavy snowfall had made the sound of his original shot seem to come from the north. To save time, I headed cross-country to Antler Mountain. As I rounded the north end, I spotted Ken and Kevin standing under a mature balsam. Projecting upward between their legs was a heavily-beamed antler.

"My buck," I uttered softly, then forcing a smile to my face to cover my disappointment.

As I walked up and began vigorously shaking my son's hand, he excitedly said, "When I shot, it dropped in its tracks."

"There seems to be a bad echo in this woods," I laughed.

"I spotted it near my stand earlier," Kevin explained, "it and a doe, yearling and fawn. They crossed our trail about 100 yards east of where I sat. Obviously smelling me, they quickly disappeared downhill toward the river."

"The buck was coming up this valley from the river when I first spotted it," Ken continued. "It stopped under this tree, only fifty yards away. I couldn't have had an easier shot."

"It's the heaviest buck we've ever taken," I observed, shaking my head. "It'll go at least 350 pounds. Nice rack, too. Another dandy for your den wall, Ken. Congratulations!"

The "cover-all-bases approach" did it again, much to my son Ken's joy.

That's cover-all-bases buck hunting.

The Nordberg deer camp, otherwise known as heaven on earth.

Though improbable, they can turn on you.

Chapter 5

Attacked by a White-tailed Buck

White-tailed bucks occasionally use their antlers to rub bark from trunks of live trees to create visible signposts of breeding ranges. The primary function of their antlers, however, is to gain mastery over other bucks via battle (shoving matches); to gain the highest possible rank in the local hierarchy of bucks. Antlers (fulcrums for directing bodily strength against other bucks) provide a means of establishing which of two bucks is physically superior, thence socially superior.

White-tailed bucks are most aggressive toward one another from velvet-shedding to antler shedding, September through early January. This is the period during which the male sex hormone, testosterone, is at its highest blood level. Testosterone and buck tempers peak about the time does first begin experiencing estrus (in November in most regions). Bucks are most dangerous while with does in estrus, especially dominant breeding bucks. If caught (uncommon), lesser bucks that dare to approach breeding does accompanied by dominant bucks face certain injury or death.

As aggressive as white-tailed bucks are among their own kind, they rarely attack humans. During hunting seasons, despite the effects of testosterone, bucks are most concerned with survival—maintaining safe distances about human hunters. This is not true of bucks that for one reason or another have no fear of humans, notably tame or pen-raised whitetails. Such bucks are known to unleash their testosterone-induced fury on their keepers. I know of three owners of pen-raised whitetails who have been severely gored by their pet bucks. One Minneapolis Area man was killed by such a buck only last fall.

Jene and I study and photograph a great number of whitetails in the course of a year, many of which have become tame in our presence. Moreover, we invariably jump at any opportunity to study and photograph dominant bucks accompanying does in estrus. Though very cautious while photographing whitetails today, during our early years we unwittingly tempted fate now and then, and as might be expected, we had a few scares.

Take the late October morning I was seated on a stump, intently studying a group of feeding Wisconsin whitetails through the view-finder of a video camera. A feisty 2-1/2 year-old buck, obviously spoiling for a fight, slipped up behind me, unobserved, and jabbed my back with a tine. Thinking my partner was pulling a prank, poking me with a stick, I reached back and gave the sharp object a shove. The next think I knew I was rolling across the ground. Only a week later, while walking toward my partner who was video-taping a dominant buck accompanying a doe in estrus, an 8-pointer unexpectedly rushed up behind me and took a swipe at the small of my back. In either case I was only slightly bruised, and thanks to unusual speed and nimble tree climbing, the hostile bucks soon began searching for more challenging opponents.

One January 1st some years later, Jene and I slipped up on two adult bucks vying for the opportunity to breed a jittery Wisconsin doe. Before we knew it, we were right in the middle of the fracas. As we held our breaths, nonetheless making frequent use of our cameras, the thoroughly enraged dominant buck, a nine-pointer with erect neck hairs that made it look like a male lion, repeatedly charged a larger 10-pointer, sometimes sweeping past within five yards of where we kneeled behind trees. So fearsome were its charges that the ten-pointer and the doe's terrified yearling buck and fawn began scattering in terror each time the dominant buck merely uttered a threatening grunt and/or took a step toward them. Upon finally realizing this enraged buck could blindly turn on us as well, Jene and I retreated from the area at our first opportunity (while the dominant buck was again charging toward the 10-pointer).

This furious buck's neck hairs were erect, giving it a lion-like appearance.

During the long trip home that day, we decided it was time to create some rules for personal safety while photographing rampaging bucks (while not sitting in a tree or carrying a weapon). Drawing from our considerable experience with wild and tame whitetails, we adopted the following guidelines:

1. From September through early January, be cautious of antlered bucks, especially dominant bucks characterized by aggressive behavior, wet and/ or wrinkled fur on the sides of their heads and necks and arched tails. In this

case "cautious" means, "approach no nearer than 50 yards, keep an eye on the buck and be constantly ready to move quickly away or climb a tree."

2. Be especially cautious when near any antlered buck that has obviously identified you but does not exhibit alarm (it does not snort, raise its tail with white rump and tail hairs erect and/or move away). If it remains near, stalks nearer, grunts (utters a low, guttural bleat) and/or appears unusually bold, wild-eyed, agitated or spoiling for a fight, move cautiously away, keeping an eye on the buck until out of sight, and be ready to quickly climb a tree.

3. If unexpectedly caught very near an aggressive buck and its antlers are lowered, tines directed toward your body, tines perhaps even actually touching your body, immediately act submissive or meek. Do nothing that may be considered a challenge. Remain silent. Make no sudden moves. Keep your head and eyes lowered, arms hanging loosely at your sides. Very slowly and very cautiously back away. Slowly step behind an adjacent tree, if available. Slowly climb the tree, if possible. If a tree is not immediately available, do not turn and run. Do not wave your arms. Do not yell. Do not make eye contact with the buck. Do not throw objects at the buck. Do not hit the buck with anything. Do not touch any part of the buck with your hands, especially its antlers. Above all, do not attempt to push the buck away, especially its antlers.

The wisdom of guideline No. 3 became well-proven some years later. Jene and I were photographing a herd of wintering whitetails in a limestone bluff area of western Wisconsin. Shortly before sunset on that fateful day, I whispered to Jene, "It's almost time to quit and I'm out of film. I'm heading down to our truck to smoke my pipe. If the light holds, I might try photographing deer signs in the cornfield next to the truck."

"I'll start down in about fifteen minutes," Jene said.

Shortly after I departed, unknown to me, a tumultuous battle suddenly broke out between the two largest bucks of the wintering area, one a twelve-pointer weighing about 325 pounds and the other a ten-pointer weighing about 300 pounds. Taking advantage of this rare photographic opportunity, Jene quickly stalked near and began shooting the action. After about two minutes of pushing, the out-classed ten-pointer was forced back three steps. Thus vanquished, it disengaged its antlers and began slowly walking away, downhill. Upon snapping one last picture of the victorious 12-pointer, which hadn't moved from the site of battle, Jene turned and headed toward the truck.

Shortly, she spotted the 10-pointer heading in her direction. Pulling an ear of corn from her pocket (we often use corn to create opportunities to photograph wintering whitetails at short range), Jene stopped and offering it to the loser, thinking the buck might walk up and take the corn from her hand as it had done a time or two before. Instead, the buck batted the ear from her hand with an antler and continued forward, finally pressing its antlers to her chest. As Jene meekly backed away, she suddenly found

Moments after this tumultuous battle ended, the smaller buck (left) challenged Jene. Fortunately, she knew what to do.

herself pinned against a fence.

White-tailed bucks commonly press their antlers against the antlers of other bucks when challenging them to engage in battle. If the challenged opponent is inclined to fight, it will return the gesture, the battle immediately beginning. If not inclined to fight, it will cautiously back away, careful to avoid banging its antlers against those of the challenger. Sometimes a reluctant opponent will lick the face of the challenger before backing off, submissive behavior akin to saying, "I give."

"I did not push back," Jene breathlessly related a few minutes later. "Remembering what happened to you that day you were sitting on that stump, I didn't dare. When I found my back against the fence, my mind went back to what I had just observed: when the smaller buck submitted, gave up, by backing away, the bigger buck stopped pushing and shoving. I quietly began backing downhill, the fence on one side of me and the wild-eyed buck on the other. After about twenty seconds of this, the buck removed its antlers from my chest and eyed me a moment. It then turned and walked away. With that, I ran to the truck."

As I write this, I still shudder to think of what might have happened if Jene had not recognized the danger of pushing the buck's antlers away from her chest. Though it is highly unlikely you will ever find yourself in similar straits, should it happen, respond exactly as Jene did. It could save your life.

Chapter 6

Lyme Disease

Early smptoms of Lyme disease include a rash, flu-like symptions, malaise, fatigue, headaches and painful muscles and joints. In some cases, there are no early symptoms. In early stages Lyme disease is difficult to diagnose, serilogical testing unrealiable. If untreated, later symptoms include meningitis, Bell's palsy, encephalitis, abnomalities of the heart and chronic arthritis.

North American white-tailed deer (and some other wild animals) are commonly infected with Lyme disease. It is spread from deer to deer by a small tick. Whitetail hunters hunt where these ticks are common and handle infected deer infested with them. Whitetail hunters are thus at high risk for contracting Lyme disease. It is therefore important for whitetail hunters to understand how to prevent being infected with this dread disease, how to determine whether the disease may or may not have been contracted and how to cure it.

Three kinds of ticks are known to carry Lyme disease: 1) the deer or bear tick found in the Northeast and Midwest, 2) the black-legged tick found in the South and 3) the Western or California black-legged tick found in the West. The adult males of these ticks are dark brown to black in color; the females brick-red or orange-brown with a black spot near the head. They are quite small, about the size of a sesame seed.

Not all ticks of this description are infected with the spyrochete, Borrelia burgdorferi, that causes Lyme disease Depending on the geographic region, as few as 10% and as many as 80% are carriers. Moreover, such ticks must be attached to the skin 12–24 hours before they can begin transmitting the disease (lending to easy prevention), but because such ticks are very small and their bites are painless, an attached tick may not be noticed for several days.

From the date of the transmission of this disease, early symptons do not usually appear for a period of 3–33 days, in some cases not at all. The most common early symptom, occurring in about 80% of infections, is a solid or ring-like red rash or spot about the site of the bite. 1–4 or more inches in diameter. The redness, which may be painless, painful. itchy and/or hot to the touch, can spread or appear on other parts of the body. It may disappear after a few days or persist more than a month. Other early symptoms are listed above.

The most obvious sign of a possible or impending infection is an attached tick of the above description. Once found, it is prudent to remove it as quickly as possible. The safest and most practical means of removing the tick is to grasp it firmly at its head end with a tweezers with well curved tips and pull it gently off (don't jerk it off). Try not to squeeze its body. Squeezing the body may force fluids, including lyme disease spyrochettes, into the wound. After removal, wash the site with soap and water and apply an antiseptic. Place the tick in a small container and mark the date on the outside. If early symptoms appear, see your physician right away, and take your tick with you. Diagnosis being as difficult as it is, your tick will lend greatly to making a positive diagnosis.

If diagnosed and treated with antibiotics (tetracycline, etc.) early, the disease can usually be cured within 10–30 days without much risk of later complications.

Prevention, of course, is the best medicine. Using the following four precautions, you are unlikely to become infected with Lyme disease even where infected ticks are fairly common.

First, wear tick-proof clothing. Wear outer clothing that fits snuggly around your ankles, waist, wrists and neck. Tuck you pant cuffs inside your stockings or boots or tie or tape them firmly to the outside. Gloves and a headnet tucked inside your shirt will help to keep ticks off otherwise exposed skin and hair. In warm weather wear a fresh set of outer clothing daily. Store worn clothing sealed in a plastic bag. To keep infected ticks from spreading into your home, either spray clothing sealed in plastic bags with 0.5 % permethrin, a tick insecticide (don't wear clothing treated in this way—permethrin should not be applied to the skin) or dump your bags directly into your washing machine after it is filled with hot soapy water.

Second, use a tick repellent. Apply a repellent containing DEET on clothing and exposed skin (not eyes and lips) and/or apply permethrin to the outer surfaces of your clothing only.

Third, at the end of each day of hunting, inspect your body thoroughly for ticks. To make certain your back is free of ticks, use a mirror or the buddy system. To make certain your hair is not hiding ticks, comb it throroughly.

Fourth, do not cut yourself while field dressing a freshly killed deer. Take your time and use a short-bladed knife. Whereas I've seen no literature that establishes the fact that Lyme disease can be transmitted via a fresh cut bathed with the blood of an infected whitetail, I think it is only prudent to avoid this likely avenue of infection. If you have a cut on your hand before beginning this task, it would be advisable to wear rubber surgical gloves or ask someone else to field dress your deer.

Epilogue

Cry of the Fawn

While editing this book, the plaintive cry of a fawn being killed by a pair of adult wolves 150 yards from my camp at 10:30AM, July 24, 1994 frequently came to mind. A week after this incident occurred, I removed one of the fawn's molars, an incisor and a dewclaw (see photo) from deer-hair-filled wolf droppings a short distance from the kill site.

Various wolf studies and personal observations of less abundant wolves in Aitkin County, Minnesota (over a period of twenty years) indicate wolves do not ordinarily hunt whitetails during summer months, and when they do hunt whitetails, they generally hunt at night. Typically, the hair and skeletal parts found in summer droppings of Aitkin County wolves were those of various rodents (from mice to beavers).

Admittedly, grouse and hare populations of my Canadian Border study area are presently as low as they can be, but this is certainly not true of vole and beaver populations. Voles (short-tailed mice) are often seen scurrying almost everywhere in this area and I've never been in a region inhabited by as many beavers. I think the wolves of this region have simply grown accustomed to eating venison year-around.

The whitetails of this four-square-mile area have not numbered more than ten per square mile (November) over the past five years. During November, we Nordbergs have harvested 0.075–1.0 adult buck per square-mile annually (3–4 bucks). As close as I can figure, the wolves have harvested 1.5–1.75 fawns per square-mile annually, 6–7 of the 9–13 fawns annually produced by 9 adult does. They have also taken an additional 0.75 adult deer per square-mile annually (three adult deer per year, usually killed in yarding areas). The wolves are thus taking about 25% of the deer in my study area annually (in my Aitkin County study area, 1970–1989, wolves harvested 3.8–7.7% of deer annually, primarily during winter months).

Unable to take significant numbers of adult deer except while whitetails are weakened by starvation in winter, less-fleet fawns are principle prey of the wolves of my Canadian Border study area during summer months. During the past two months, Jene and I found portions of bones (fresh) from at least three fawns (other than the one mentioned above) that were killed by these wolves (identified by their tracks and droppings at kill sites) within the four-square-mile area surrounding our campsite. Virtually all wolf droppings found in this area this past summer contained hair and often skeletal parts of whitetails (unworn teeth identifying fawn kills). At the present rate of fawn predation, I doubt more than one fawn of four in this area will survive to see the first snow of November.

Whereas this rough sampling may not reflect the extent to which wolves are preying on whitetails elsewhere in northern Minnesota, and whereas it may not reflect a relative abundance of wolves in this or any other area of the state, the fact that normally nocturnal wolves are now regularly hunting by day throughout northern Minnesota strongly suggests they are not only over-abundant, but, as a result, they are short of food.

Only hunger attributable to a poor crop of wild berries will induce normally elusive black bears to raid garbage cans during daylight hours in metropolitan areas such as Duluth, places they would never dare appear otherwise, even at night. Hunger, I believe, attributable to a fawn population no longer adequate enough to support current numbers of Minnesota wolves, is forcing these normally-nocturnal carnivores to hunt by day. This should come as no surprise. As was well proven on Isle Royale some years ago, completely protected wolves are incapable of maintaining population levels consistant with the carrying capacities of their ranges.

Fawn teeth and dewclaw removed from wolf droppings—killed by wolves July 24, 1994

The trouble is, Americans who insist upon providing wolves with the cruel legacy of absolute protection have thus far made it impossible to reduce Minnesota wolf numbers to levels that will allow wolf country whitetails to recover to former (pre-1968) levels. It has been suggested sportshunting (of whitetails) should be banned (in this region) as a means of providing wolves with adequate food. How long would it take before unrestricted wolves would overwhelm additional whitetails provided by such a measure? I'd safely venture 2–4 years. What then? Allow increasingly-abundant wolves to whittle away at whitetail numbers until they are reduced to 1971 levels? Whitetails of this region still haven't recovered from the terrible winters of 1968–71 and, under current circumstances, it is doubtful they ever will. When it finally becomes manefestly evident wolves are starving, that Minnesota's much-cherished white-tailed deer and other game can no longer support their overwhelming numbers, what will we do then? Use taxpayer's money to feed them?

Don't get me wrong. I much admire wolves. I am still in awe each time I see them near or hear their howls. Moreover, if not over-abundant, they actually benefit whitetails. It is because of my feelings toward these wonderful creatures that I dare to suggest our Minnesota wolves need biologically-sound management, and soon (vehemently opposed a few years ago when offered by the Minnesota Department of Natural Resources). Judging from what I have observed over the past five years, I believe our wolves are on the brink of serious starvation and needless suffering. Their principle prey, white-tailed deer, are needlessly suffering right now. Neither of these magnificent animals deserves such a fate.

Many Americans are inclined to support our current wolf protection policies, believing they will thus someday experience the thrill of hearing the mournful howl of a wolf. I wish these same Americans could also hear the cry of a white-tailed fawn being killed by a wolf. For the sake of both our wolves and deer, we could stand a little less of either sound.

Good hunting, my friend,

Doc

Other valuable hunting guides by Dr. Ken Nordberg
(prices effective September, 1994)

Whitetail Hunter's Almanac, 6th Edition—$8.95
An advanced guide to hunting whitetails of deep forests, brushlands, wetlands, mountains, high hills and bluffs, farmlands, prairies, urban areas and wolf country. Included is a chapter entitled, "New Tips That Triple Success," the final tip another of Doc's new, amazingly-effective hunting methods (100% as of this date), "The Gentle Nudge."

Whitetail Hunter's Almanac, 5th Edition—$8.95
A scientifically-based guide to new and improved methods of hunting whitetails on foot. Featured are portable stump hunting, mile-a-day still-hunting, selective trailing, trailing wounded deer, improved stalking and adult-buck-effective drives—all applicable to bowhunting. Portable stump hunting, a new hunting method, will double or triple your success whatever your current favorite hunting method.

Whitetail Hunter's Almanac, 4th Edition—$8.95
A scientifically-based guide to more than 200 signs of white-tailed deer and the "sign method" of hunting whitetails. A thorough understanding of deer signs is the only reliable means to achieving regular hunting success, whatever hunting method is used.

Whitetail Hunter's Almanac, 3rd Edition—$8.95
A scientifically-based guide to "mobile stand hunting"—the deadliest of hunting methods. This hunting method counters the ability of today's adult whitetails to identify and begin regularly avoiding hunters using stands within 24–48 hours. Also provided are guidelines for 21 different stand sites, including physical features, positioning, most productive periods and special precautions.

Whitetail Hunter's Almanac, 2nd Edition—$8.95
A perennial favorite among whitetail hunters everywhere. A scientifically-evolved guide to hunting adult bucks only during the five phases of the rut, September through December.

Whitetail Hunter's Almanac, 1st Edition—$8.95
More than an introduction and primer to whitetail hunting. This ever-popular book provides tips and instructions for almost anything to do with whitetail hunting, including scouting, sign analysis and all popular hunting methods, field dressing, measuring record-book antlers, home butchering, cooking venison and much more.

Whitetail Sign Guides—$8.95
For scouting and hunting, 12 quick and easy-to-use, laminated field guide cards with a non-glare poly-pocket covering the following: identifying deer, their ranges and key range elements via tracks, droppings, beds,

antler rubs and ground scrapes, 15 productive stand sites, the five phases of the rut, how to recover wounded deer, field dressing, predicting the timing of whitetail movements (including midday movements triggered by special weather conditions) and more. Using by more than 70,000 hunters today.

Do-It-Yourself Black Bear Baiting and Hunting—$8.95
A complete, scientifically-based guide to hunting trophy-class black bears. Written for beginners, veteran do-it-yourselfers and guides. Featured are well-proven, step-by-step instructions for scouting, baiting and hunting tough-to-hunt, rarely-seen bruins weighing more than 300 pounds. Doc really knows bears. Using the exact methods described in this book, he took two record-book bears with his bow on his last two hunts.

To order, send check or money order (U.S. funds) plus $1.10 ($1.34 Canada) for postage & mailer per 1–2 books and/or Sign Guide sets ordered (MN residents add $.57 tax per book or Sign Guide set) to: Dr. Ken Nordberg, 6912 Logan Ave. N., Brooklyn Center, MN 55430.

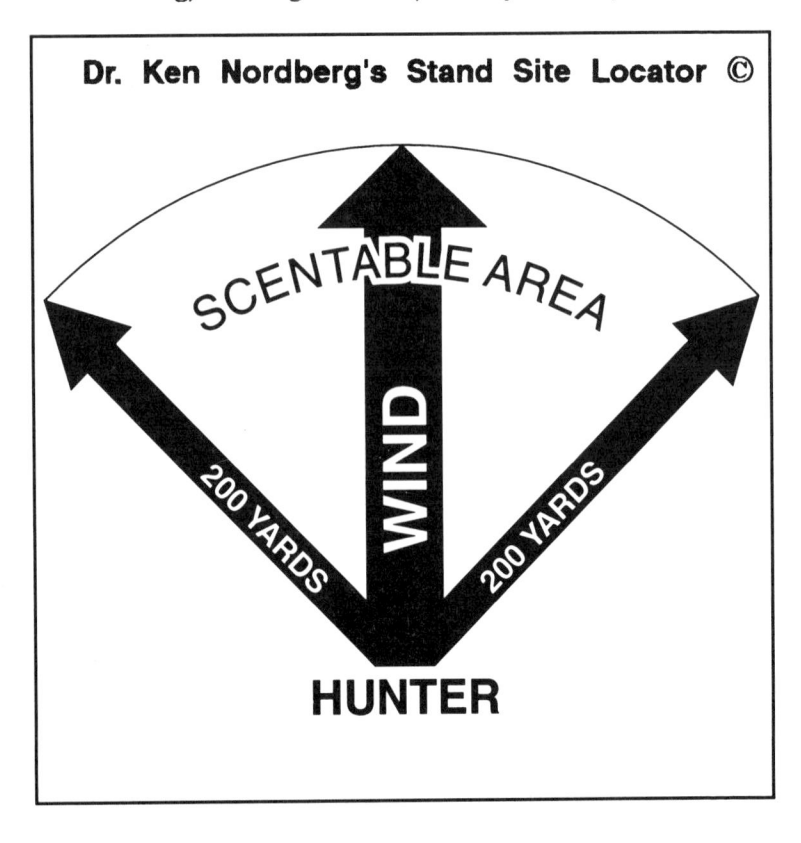